Praise for *I See You!*

"If you could build a person using contagious energy, radical empathy, ready humor, and business savvy, you would get a replica of Erin Diehl, and somehow, she's managed to capture that within the pages of this book. In *I See You!* Erin provides you with her time-tested methods for maximizing your energy so you can maximize the good you create for your team, your family, and, most importantly, yourself."

–Cy Wakeman, *New York Times* best-selling author,
keynote speaker, and drama researcher

"*I See You!* by Erin Diehl is a revelation for leaders in a world hungry for authenticity and genuine connection. Her insights resonate deeply, offering a blueprint to create passion-struck cultures where individuals flourish. A groundbreaking read that challenges traditional leadership norms and introduces a new era of purpose-driven, empathetic leadership."

–John R. Miles, author of *Passion Struck* and host
of the *Passion Struck* podcast

"If you are a leader experiencing burnout and need a pick-me-up, grab this book now. *I See You!* is bursting with the laughter, empathy, and great storytelling that will give you the power to change your habits and the way you see the world."

–Claude Silver, chief heart officer, VaynerX

"This book is such a puntastic delight! Informed by her self-declared doctorate in fun, Erin Diehl's positivity and humor are exactly what you need in your life and in your organization. Humor is the best medicine! This is the most fun you will ever have reading a leadership book."

–Chris Do, founder & host of the top-twenty marketing podcast *The Futur*

"Erin created a perfect book for perfectionists in recovery who want to start their transition and go from 'Type A' to 'Type A-dventurous.'"

–Gaby Natale, triple Emmy-winning journalist, speaker, and best-selling author

"This book is such an enjoyable read about how you can energize yourself and others. You can't lead others effectively unless you are powerfully leading yourself first, and Erin shows us how to do exactly that through the stories, lessons, and activities that she shares throughout."

–Simon Alexander Ong, best-selling author of *Energize* and international keynote speaker

"This isn't just another leadership book; it's your secret weapon. With every page turned, you'll gain the insights to transform conflict into collaboration, hurdles into stepping stones, and chaos into creativity. Erin's unique blend of humor and heart will have you saying, 'Where has this book been my whole life?'"

–Judi Holler, keynote speaker and best-selling author of *Fear Is My Homeboy*

I SEE YOU!

A LEADER'S GUIDE TO ENERGIZING YOUR
TEAM THROUGH RADICAL EMPATHY

I SEE YOU!

ERIN DIEHL

GREENLEAF
BOOK GROUP PRESS

Published by Greenleaf Book Group Press
Austin, Texas
www.gbgpress.com

Distributed by Greenleaf Book Group

For ordering information or special discounts for bulk purchases, please contact Greenleaf Book Group at PO Box 91869, Austin, TX 78709, 512.891.6100.

Design and composition by Greenleaf Book Group and Anna Jordan
Cover design by Greenleaf Book Group and Anna Jordan

Publisher's Cataloging-in-Publication data is available.

Print ISBN: 979-8-88645-146-7

eBook ISBN: 979-8-88645-147-4

To offset the number of trees consumed in the printing of our books, Greenleaf donates a portion of the proceeds from each printing to the Arbor Day Foundation. Greenleaf Book Group has replaced over 50,000 trees since 2007.

Printed in the United States of America on acid-free paper

24 25 26 27 28 29 30 31   10 9 8 7 6 5 4 3 2 1

First Edition

To Marianne, thank you for
guiding me to write this book.

To John and Jackson, my angels on Earth.
I love you, and I see you—always and forever.

Contents

Preface

As an improv comedy expert, facilitator, and podcast host who has taught over 35,000 people to chicken dance, spoken onstage with former president Barack Obama, and helped thousands of people improve their workday through experiential learning workshops, I had an entirely different book in mind. You were going to hear tips and tricks on how improv can help you be a better presenter, communicator, networker, and leader. I was going to bore you to tears with case study after case study of teams who have used improv training to help them be more cohesive, allowing "synergy" and lots of "cross-functional communication."

We will now refer to the other book as *that book*. *That book* is gone—lost, out the door with buzz words like *core competencies* and *out of pocket*. That book is dead because the new version is alive and kicking.

I didn't choose to write this book. This book chose to write me. I know what you're thinking: *Who is this chick?* Before you think I'm going to get out my crystals, light a scented candle, and turn on some meditation music, let me explain (she says as she casually puts the citrine stick and volcano candle from Anthropology in her desk drawer and turns up the new Taylor Swift album).

In the year 2022, I broke. I cracked. I hit my bottom.

The three pairs of Ps

You know the saying *what goes up must come down*? I was on the flip side of that cliché: What goes down must come up. You'll find that I love alliteration (and acronyms), and well, this time in my life could not have alliterated more. This was my period of paired Ps: *perpetually pivoting, people pleasing,* and *perceived pain.*

PERPETUAL PIVOTING

In 2020, I had no choice but to pivot my completely in-person professional development company—seemingly overnight—into something I wasn't sure could work. In a matter of just a few weeks, we became a completely virtual business to keep our doors open. And by doors, I mean our Zoom meeting room. We had no online presence at the time, and each day felt like an episode of *Survivor*. I felt naked, afraid, and hungry for a time when we didn't feel so exposed and so . . . tired! I wanted off the island, but I wanted to be victorious at the same time. The wild wilderness that was the global pandemic required pivot after pivot to innovate our way through. Adopting the notion that this was the new normal was never an option for me. Owning a business that required human-to-human connection to provide our services made staying indoors and closed off from human beings extremely difficult. And, to be blunt, it was downright depressing.

When you hear the word *pivot*, you normally think of one big change that shifts you into a new way of being. That wasn't the case for us, and I began to think about the word *pivot* as a continuous practice, one that not only shifts you into a new way of being but opens your eyes to all the ways there are *to be*. Even with this concept top of mind, I still lived in constant fight or flight mode. *Will we make it? When are we going to have to do something completely different? Is all this worth it?*

After pivoting for three solid years, our business finally achieved a P&L report that didn't have as much red on it as my face during my Accutane teenage years. Still, my fight or flight mode did not have an off switch, and I only knew this way of existing. Pivot, pivot, pivot. Worry, worry, worry. Repeat, repeat, repeat.

PEOPLE PLEASING

Enter P pair part deux. I have always been a people pleaser, but 2020 added a new element: I had just given birth to a miracle baby boy. As a new mom, a hamster on a wheel of fight or flight when it came to pivoting my business, and a human being who has deep bonds with those around me—I was trying to please everyone. My son, my husband, my team, my dad, my mom (who was recovering from a stroke), my clients, my neighbors, my online community, my dog . . . the list goes on.

The one person whom I did not please and gave zero effort to? Myself. I was drained, burned out, and depleted mentally and physically. But instead of stopping and resting, I kept going and pushing. I did this day after day, until the third P came into the picture.

PERCEIVED PAIN

I'm not talking about when you accidentally stub your toe and it stings for a good ten minutes, or when you hit your funny bone (which is not funny) and the pain lingers for a solid five. I'm talking about chronic pain, deeply rooted pain that found its home in my back. This pain caused me to cry at night. It was pain that doctors couldn't diagnose through X-rays or blood work. It was pain that didn't go away after each new chiropractor gave it their best crack. This pain stood up to acupuncture visits, cupping appointments, and dry needling sessions.

The physical pain made itself known because I hadn't taken the time to know its counterpart: my emotional pain. The deep-rooted, unprocessed emotions that I had been hiding from were blocking me from knowing my inner guidance system and truly becoming the woman I wanted to be.

It dawned on me that I hadn't processed the many rounds of IVF that I went through to conceive our son, the stroke that almost killed my mother, or the pandemic that took away an unimaginable number of lives and almost squashed my identity and my business. I wasn't able to see myself, hadn't processed any of this emotional pain; instead, I dissociated by diving into work, motherhood, and other people's problems. I hid from it at night with a dirty martini, a glass or two of wine, or a bad reality television show that made my mind go numb. Now I have the language of *process* and *dissociate*, but at the time, throwing myself into everything besides the problem felt normal—expected, even.

I thought Tylenol, Motrin, stretching, and physical therapy were reasonable methods to deal with the pain, but it had other plans. It persisted until one day, a mentor told me about Gabor Maté's *When the Body Says No*. I read the final chapter of the book on a red-eye flight home after keynote speaking at a conference. In that moment, everything clicked—like what you see in the movies but without the background music or a zoom-in on my face. I realized that my body was screaming at me because I hadn't listened to any of its whispers. I hadn't given myself permission to feel the pain that came with almost losing the business with a mission that is my life's purpose, almost losing the woman who gave me life, and almost not having the opportunity to give life to my son. There's something particularly haunting about all of these *almost*s that has kept me subconsciously angry, and it's this: I hadn't allowed myself to feel any of it.

I closed the book on that plane and cried in the dark in my seat next to a stranger who was most likely *very* confused. OK, I didn't just cry. I sobbed. I'm talking big, heavy, Kim Kardashian ugly-cry tears.

I had found the root of my pain, and now it was time for me to get to work. I drove home from the airport that night determined and ready. By tomorrow, I would heal, and the pain would go away. I would be free because I had found the cure.

Then tomorrow came, and so did the next tomorrow, the next tomorrow, and the next. How do you heal years of unprocessed emotions; years of putting energy into everyone else except you; years of anger, sadness, and loss? You give it time. You go into a healing cocoon. You lock yourself in a closet every morning and journal.

Speaking of closets, I called this the Marie Kondo method for processing emotions. Marie Kondo had a Netflix show about home organization in which she helped homeowners declutter and eliminate what no longer sparks joy. In a similar way, I considered each specific event in my brain as its own closet: one closet for my IVF journey, one closet for my journey into motherhood, one closet for the loss of our in-person business as we knew it, and one closet for the near loss of my mother. Each closet had several drawers holding unprocessed emotions waiting to be acknowledged, felt, and released. And each drawer looked like the junkiest junk drawer you have in your home—the one with the car keys, phone chargers, sunglasses, papers from your kid's preschool, rubber bands. You know the one.

So I went into each mind closet and decluttered, one drawer at a time. This took time, energy, and several boxes of Kleenex. I thanked the emotions that no longer served me and let them go. Newer, more positive emotions took their place. Although this sounds cathartic and charming, I didn't want to leave my house. And since I'm here to tell the truth, there were some moments I didn't want to be alive.

Living with the three paired Ps was the hardest, most isolating time in my life. The funny thing is that, once I processed the emotions and finally had some more organized mind closets, most of my back pain vanished. Once I shifted my focus to healing my emotional pain instead of my physical pain, the physical pain didn't scream at me anymore. It still creeps up when I fall back into old patterns, but I am now mostly pain free and am enjoying a new phase of life with a new set of Ps: purpose, priorities, and peace.

I now have a sense of inner freedom that I've never felt before. I see myself for who I am and who I can be. This freedom allows me to say "I love myself" and mean it. I practice self-care. I show up for myself first so that I can show up for others. I look at my failures as gifts and have tools to get myself out of the funkiest of funks. I also have a spiritual connection with my truest, highest self, as well as a deep connection with my Inner Guide (to you, this may be God, the Universe, or Source Energy).

The connection

This connection with my Inner Guide is the driving force for this book (not *that book*) coming to life. We all have access to our Inner Guide; it is just up to us to take time to be still and listen. Through this guidance, I have surrendered to what I am here on this Earth to do, and through that surrender, I have been reborn.

In that rebirth, I have found a deep connection with myself and a deeper understanding of how the fear of failure, people pleasing, and chronic stress play a role in how we show up in our day-to-day lives, especially in our workplace. The pandemic created a giant spotlight on how leaders show up not only for their teams but for themselves, especially when placed under constant pressure. Let's look at some of the statistics that prove this point even further.

According to Gallup's *State of the Global Workplace* report, workplace stress reached an all-time high in 2022, amid post-pandemic fears and stubborn inflation. Another 2022 study conducted by the American Psychiatric Association shows that three-quarters of American adults said they have experienced health impacts due to stress, including headaches, fatigue, anxiety, and depression.

An article for Deloitte titled "The C-Suite's Role in Well-Being" discusses a study showing that one-third of executives are constantly struggling with fatigue and stress and with feelings of being overwhelmed, lonely, or depressed. This stress felt by managers cascades to their employees, impacting well-being, retention, and performance.

In an April 25, 2023, article for *Forbes*, Garen Staglin describes how "managers can trigger anxiety in their employers through unusual or erratic actions, emotional volatility, excessive pessimism, and ignoring people's emotions. Managers that withdraw or are more hotheaded have teams that are 62 percent more likely to leave their jobs and 56 percent more likely to stop participating."

This leadership illusion to keep up with the fast-paced business evolution and always be *on* leaves little room for upkeep and off switches. As leaders, we prioritize the needs of the business and the reactionary needs of employees and forget to put ourselves first. This lack of energy input into ourselves causes a lack of connection not only with our highest self but in our relationships. This includes relationships with the people we lead, our teams, our organizations, and the communities we belong to.

The new vision

Once the connection was made, I realized why this book was needed and why it was needed now. This book is for the leaders, parents, partners, friends, siblings, daughters, sons who put everyone else in their life first. This book is *the* resource for you, the leader, who is suffering in a leadership role and needs actionable, tangible steps to take to make sure that YOU are taken care of first.

Don't worry: I see you. By reading and applying these fundamentals, you will place energy into yourself first, create long-lasting impact on the people you lead, and magnetize a company culture and workplace beyond your wildest dreams.

I will take your hand and guide you through a journey of self-exploration using laughter, levity, and positivity. I'll help you hold up a mirror so you can see yourself clearly. The result is a newfound sense of self-love, inner peace, and a new way of seeing the world. Through this newfound vision, you will be able to see yourself differently and turn your newfound positive internal energy outward. This electric force will attract others and magnetize true connection. These new connections will be vibrant and colorful and help you to see the positive force within others but, more importantly, the positive force within yourself.

I will be right here beside you, as your personal cheerleader, professional development bestie, and professor, guiding you to become the visionary you were meant to be. Because, in the end, *I see you* means that we all see the light in ourselves and can help others see their light, too. What a better world to live in, and what a beautiful sight to truly see.

Welcome to Energy U

"Love yourself first and everything else falls in line. You really have to love yourself to get anything done in this world."

—Lucille Ball, according to Google

Hello, new student and new friend! Welcome to your first day at Energy U. I'm so glad that you've decided to invest in yourself. You will find that many people who attend Energy U graduate with honors. They hold a prestigious degree and do wonderful things in the world.

There are hundreds of thousands of famous and well-respected alumni in the world (all who wish to remain anonymous). However, you can easily spot them if you try. These are the people who are putting love into themselves so that they can give to their teams, communities, families, and organizations. They are the people who can solve problems with ease, brighten rooms, and lead teams and people to be their highest and greatest selves.

Now, before you get overwhelmed and stop reading, know this: If you apply yourself, listen, learn, and do the homework, the outcome will be far greater than you could have ever imagined. You will find that the energy you put into the time you spend here will equal the energy you get out of it. It's that simple. We have a tried-and-true curriculum that will guide you using laughter and practical application. Think of this place as a practical, real-life internship that embraces you with comedy and comfort, providing you with the ultimate reward of inner peace and calm. (Imagine adding those things to your résumé under *special skills*!)

Meet your professor

Now, before we go any further, let me start by introducing myself. I'm Erin Diehl, lead professor of this magnet school, Energy U. Keep in mind that I don't have a doctorate in physics (in fact, never even taken the class), but I *do* have a doctorate in fun. I call this degree my PHD (pretty huge Diehl), because this school is punstoppable, and it just so happens that I have a pretty punny last name. But I'm not just any professor. I'm a cool professor (think Amy Poehler in *Mean Girls*), a bit wacky (think Eddie Murphy in *The Nutty Professor*), and I can help you change the way you see yourself and the world. Pretty cool, huh?

I am also not an eye doctor (or a doctor at all)! There are no vision tests, but I do assess the way you see yourself and the world around you during your time here. There will not be a vision chart, nor will there be one of those machines where they make you stick your chin on a strap and it shoots a rapid blast of air into your retina. There are no X-rays, and there is absolutely no dilation, so you can set the cardboard sunglasses aside. Now that you know who I am not, let's get into who I am.

I am your guide through this lively journey. If you stick with me, I'll promise to give you all the tangible tips and tricks you need to create more self-love, lead with empathy, and magnetize a culture and network so attractive that it makes Brad Pitt look like the ugliest man in the world.

Maybe you're reading this and thinking to yourself, *I love the culture and community I currently have. Nothing needs to change!* That's awesome. But, my friend, there is always room for improvement. Or perhaps you are seeking a connection back to yourself or a deeper, more authentic connection with others. Well, I've got you! Or maybe you're overwhelmed and need quick digestible tips on how to attract the things you want at work and in life. I'm your gal. Or equally as important, maybe you are reentering the workforce and are looking for new ways to show up more confidently. Friend, I'm going to blow your mind. Whatever the case, know that I don't take my role as your professor lightly, although I *will* shine light on you and your amazing capabilities and help you see the magnetic force within you so you can become the selfless leader you were meant to be.

What is Energy U?

Speaking of seeing, let me help you visualize what Energy U is all about and how we came to be.

When was your birthday?

Oh! I love that day. That was *the* day we were founded, and little did you know that, on that day, you were automatically enrolled into this magnet school.

Now, not to sound ageist, but you started working on the prerequisites for Energy U many years ago. I know, I know: We have a *lot* of prerequisites. It's an aggressive curriculum, but we needed you to learn, try, fail, refine, adopt, abandon, and accelerate on your own before you went all-in on Energy U.

Now you may be thinking, *Why haven't I heard about this sooner? Am I being punked? Where's Ashton Kutcher? Is there somewhere online where I can see the curriculum that I had no clue I had done until today?*

I'm so glad you asked! Here's how you find this secret hidden curriculum that you've been studying for many years: Open your phone or computer. Go to any social network, such as Facebook or Instagram. Not a social media type? Open the photos section on your phone. Examine your pictures. These are your core memories. Little did you know, you were learning the heartbeat of this curriculum this entire time! I'm sure you can look at any picture and remember how you felt in that exact moment. Go ahead, pick a picture. That picture, that moment—that was energy. That was Energy U at work! Congrats to you for being a star pupil without even realizing it. You overachiever, you!

You see, energy is all around you. You've been studying it your entire life. It's in every thought that pops into your mind, in every word you say, and in every action and interaction you have. You've been learning it since day one, but now it's time for a master class.

Starting today, your curriculum is changing. We are going to take a deeper dive into energy and what it means. We'll use that definition to pour more of it into ourselves, so we can give out more of it to our teams, communities, organizations, and families. Once we understand how this works, we will be able to see others in a different way, because we see ourselves in a completely different light. This newfound vision will show up everywhere in your life, from the teams you lead to your interactions with clients, vendors, partners, neighbors, friends, and family members. It's a tried-and-true curriculum, and if you follow it, you will be blindsided by how much your vision improves (yes, this metaphor totally makes sense). You will start magnetizing and attracting people and things into your life that feel like little slices of heaven, all because you are doing the work internally and placing that work externally into the world.

What is energy?

To understand our own electric currents, let's start with a cliché and define the term *energy*. According to Wikipedia (yes, we're leaning all the way into that cliché), it's "the quantitative property that is transferred to a body or to a physical system, recognizable in the performance of work and in the form of heat and light." Thank you, Wikipedia.

Energy U takes this definition and does what we do in improv: It *yes, and*s it. This means we hear what they are saying and agree to it without judgment, then add something to it. Our yes-and definition of energy is connection, the transference of light to another human being. It's vibration and being true to you, and then giving that vibrational frequency to another person. It's attracting, magnetizing, and bringing forth the goodness in others using your own vibrational output as the compass.

ENERGETIC EXPERIENCE

Here's a quick way to experience energy: Get out a sheet of paper, and write at the top *Positive Energy*. Now draw a line down the center of the paper to create two columns. On the top left, write the word *people*. On the right, write the word *emotions*. Start by writing a list of people on the left who come to mind when you think of positive energy. Go ahead, fill up the column with the list of people who bring sunshine, joy, and lots of zest to your life. I'll wait.

Now that you have a smile from ear to ear (at least that's how I picture you), write down in the right column all the emotions that come to mind when you think of these people. It could be words like *silly, goofy, creative, fun, laughter,* and *love.* Go ahead and write them down now. I'm not going anywhere.

What words come up for you? Chances are, you associate mostly positive emotions with the positive people in your life. If you have words like *cranky, negative, rude, mean,* and *unpleasant* in your emotion column, consider taking these people off your list. Of course, no one is perfect, but positive people provoke positive emotions within us. Positive people awaken something in you because they have an energetic field around them that is attractive, that makes you want to be around them. They magnetize you to their presence. Notice how your body feels doing this exercise. That feeling, that vibration, *that* is energy.

The same can be true for negative energy. Have you ever been in a waiting room for the doctor's office and there was a patient pacing back and forth? You can feel their angst and nervousness, and it's affecting the vibe of the entire room. *That* is energy. Or, dare I say, perhaps you've been waiting in line at Starbucks and you see a person who is jonesing for their morning cup of joe. They are like a dog salivating for their treat, and you can feel the anxiety go away as soon as they get that first-sip feeling. *That* is energy. Or have you ever been in a meeting and a Negative Nancy sucks all the joy out of the room like a vacuum cleaner? Everyone is cheerful and hopeful, while Nancy is just sucking up all the good air and creating a space filled with negative dust bunnies and crumbs of despair. All innovation goes out the window, and the room is left feeling stiff and stale. *That* is energy.

We've all been in situations where we can feel energy shift and sense negative and positive vibes. But what if I told you that you have a choice in how you give and receive energy? What if I told you that it all started with *you*?

Meet Upset U

As you can see, energy is ever present. We can feel energy everywhere, in everyone. Can you think of a time when you weren't emitting a positive frequency, when you were upset, rattled, or discouraged and those emotions spilled out to others? Of course you can. You're human. We have emotions, and sometimes, due to life circumstances, we go to the negative.

Perhaps you rolled out of bed after hitting snooze on your alarm clock five times this morning. Then you ran around your house as if you had hot coals under your feet trying to get ready. You slammed drawers, shot toothpaste all over the counter while trying to get it on your toothbrush, and threw your clothes all over the floor like the Tasmanian Devil while searching for that perfect pair of socks that was most definitely in the bottom of your cluttered drawer.

Since you take a bus to get to work, you hopped on the extra-crowded 151 Express and stood in the armpit of a stranger for twenty minutes as you held on for dear life with one hand and fumbled with your iPhone in the other. (It is not best practice to make eye contact with the armpit you are interlocked with!) You got to work, grabbed a coffee before racing to your desk, and prayed that your team didn't look at the clock to notice that you were indeed fifteen minutes late—again.

You sat at your desk and angrily opened your email because now you're sweating due to the coffee and winter coat that resembles a down comforter with a zipper. You angrily told off a vendor for trying to sell you something when you did *not* ask to be sold to. You had no formal plan for your day, but you picked up one of the seven Post-it notes you left out as reminders for yourself the day before and started a task.

Can you relate to Upset U? If you nodded your head to any one of these situations, I want you to know you are not alone. All of us have been Upset U at some point in our lives because, well, we are human!

Upset U is a true story—mine. This was a previous version of me. I know: You don't like to think of your professor in a negative light, but we keep it real around here. This was an exact portrayal of how I started my day every day when I first became a business owner. I grew up living in this fight or flight mode and allowed it to be my normal existence. As I ventured down the path of leading a team, managing client relationships, and starting a business from scratch, Upset Me was present on every morning commute, every workday, and every major event. Upset Me's mental and physical health was a constant roller coaster ride. Some days, she took care of herself and was on the upward slope; other days, she relied on coffee, coffee, and more coffee to get through the day. Other days, she would be on the lowest part of the ride, with no clue how she could push herself to the top and over the slump. She would push and push until her body collapsed from exhaustion. Her family and team would ride this roller coaster with her, wondering if we were going to gently climb the slope or fly through a loop each day.

I didn't love being Upset Me. However, at that time in my life, it was all I knew. I had just founded my professional development company, *improve it!*, and was trying to start a family. After several years of infertility and a team that was constantly reacting to my stress levels, I realized that Upset Me had to go. By being this reactive, frazzled shell of a person who ran from task to task throughout the day, I was resisting all the good that I could have been attracting into my life. I was resisting attracting the right clients and the right people to be a part of our team. I was also resisting the ability to become a mother. Little did I know that I had to learn to mother *myself* before I could mother anyone else.

Upset Me needed to let go of the need to control everything, the need to rush through the day, to accomplish and achieve without self-awareness of my mental or physical health. I needed to learn how to put energy into myself so I could put out the right energy to my team and the people we serve. This shift did not happen overnight, and I did not become a mother right away. However, through the eradication of Upset Me, a new person was born. Well, two, I guess, if you count my son.

Meet Upward U

Introducing the enemy of Upset U: Upward U! Instead of rolling out of bed and hitting snooze, Upward U gets up with your alarm. Upward U is excited for the morning because you've intentionally planned it the night before. You have your clothes laid out for your morning workout, get thirty minutes of exercise, and give yourself ten minutes of meditation. You start your day by creating a to-do list, because you know you need your creative time in the morning and your meetings in the afternoon. You set up your calendar with care and create boundaries with your meetings so you are not stuck in Zoom call after Zoom call or meeting after meeting every single day.

Upward U can handle problems and conflict with grace because you have calmed your mind *first*. You go through the day acknowledging and authenticating others' ideas around you. You ask questions and genuinely care about the answers, as well as the personal and professional growth of the individual you are talking to. You close out the day planning for the next, end with gratitude, and give yourself intentional downtime to reset and recharge.

Upward U has put energy into yourself first. You have figured out how to manage yourself, your own energy, and your vibrational frequency, so you can expel energy into the world that supports and acknowledges others. You have filled your own tea kettle first so you can pour into other people's cups. You have given to the most important person in your life—YOU—first.

I can officially say that Upset Me morphed into Upward Me after applying intentional effort into how I showed up for myself every day. These efforts took time to learn and were game changers in how I felt on a regular basis. These tips and tricks allowed me to show up as the best version of myself and are what I'm going to teach you during your time at Energy U.

Upset Me saw herself as stressed, overworked, and busy, whereas Upward Me is calm, balanced, and intentional. Once I made the shifts to truly see who the highest version of myself could be, my vision and perception changed. I could see the real me, the person I was meant to be. I saw my flawed, imperfect, fun, lively, flawesome (that's flawed and awesome) self—and I loved her. I wanted to make her happy so she could fulfill her life's purpose: to show others how to truly *see* themselves, too.

Are you ready to truly see the person you are now and the person you can become? It's going to take time and intentional effort, but I promise to get you there. Seeing yourself—like I see you—is the first step in magnetizing who you want around you as your team, your partners, your family, and your relationships. It's like going to the gym: You must work your vision muscle to see and recognize your own strength.

Don't worry, I'll be your professor and your personal trainer, guiding you through. You want to know the best news of all? We don't need fancy equipment, because you already have everything you need to start. That big, shiny, industrial-size machine is *your mind*. Did I just blow it!? Get ready; there is more where that came from!

Activity: Tone it up!

The Tone it up! exercises below remind you that changing the tone can change the meaning in a conversation. Perhaps today, you said a word that has a positive connotation, like *happy*. But what if you were asked to say it using a negative emotion? By changing the emotional tone, this changes the perception—the energy—of that word. When we realize that we can do this with words, we learn that we can do it with thoughts.

When we can change the tone of our inner voice to be more nurturing and loving, we can show up for ourselves differently. When we realize that we can do this for ourselves, we have more capacity and willingness to show up for others. Showing up for others can look like a smile, a salutation in an email, or a genuine "how are you?" It can mean giving the person on our team just the right words to help them get through a hard time. It can mean shifting the energy of a group from a negative brainstorm to a more productive and meaningful innovation session. The tone of our inner dialogue affects the outer dialogue, and tone is usually what is heard in conversations more than the words themselves.

The following activities are going to help us open our eyes to the power of our own energy. The solo activity is for you to do on your own before moving on. The group activity is for you to use with your team as you go through Energy U together or come back to after and teach once you have a full grasp of our curriculum. For both exercises, make sure you have established a safe space for yourself and others before starting.

continued

Solo activity

Step 1: Think of a word—any word at all. Example: *Pickles.* (Who doesn't love pickles?!)

Step 2: Say the word out loud. Example: "Pickles."

Step 3: Examine how you feel about the word. Does it have a positive or negative connotation? Example: "I love pickles. They make every sandwich better," or "I hate pickles. Why did they ruin cucumbers?"

Step 4: Now say the word again, but this time, add a negative emotion (judgmental, angry, nervous).

Step 5: Say the word again with positive emotion (joyful, excited, surprised).

Step 6: Go to the activity debrief below.

Group activity

Step 1: Have the group stand in a circle and pick one person to start. That person will say a word—any word at all. Example: "Pickles."

Step 2: Starting clockwise, the person next to person A (let's call them person B) will say a word using the last letter of the person before them. So, if the word was *pickles*, they would say a word that starts with the letter S. Person B says, "snake," so person C says a word that starts with the letter E. Allow the group to do this once around in a circle and then move on to step 3.

Step 3: Now, add a negative emotion to the last letter word game. Still using the last letter of the word before, use negative emotion to say the new word. Negative emotions can be judgmental, angry, nervous. Example: If the last word in step 2 was *elephant*, you could start this round with *tepid*, *tense*, or *tearful*.

Step 4: Still using the last letter of the word before, use positive emotions to say the next word. Example: If you finished step 3 with *stressed,* you could start this one with *delighted.*

Step 5: Move on to activity debrief.

Activity debrief

Question 1: How did it feel assigning a negative emotion to the word? Did you like the word you chose? Did assigning the negative emotion make you feel different?

Question 2: How did it feel assigning positive emotion to the word? Did you dislike the word you chose? Did assigning a positive emotion make you feel different?

Go to itserindiehl.com/resources to get your
downloadable *I See You! Guidebook.*

Your Energy U orientation wrap-up

You've learned a lot during your first day at Energy U. We really like to pack it in, right? As your professor, I am so proud and know that you have a bright future ahead. You've discovered the meaning of energy, and you've experienced it, witnessed it, and noticed the transformative power of its intentionality at work. You've realized that we can transform ourselves using intentional shifts, and those intentional shifts start by working out our greatest muscle: the mind. OK, if your brain is literally a muscle, you might need some medical attention, but I'm going to help you do some metaphorical cerebral squats.

There is no putting it off until tomorrow, no forgetting the gym shoes or getting too busy here. It's time for a deep dive, a mental workout, a brain sweat sesh. But before we get to it, make sure you take the time to really digest and absorb the activities here. There are no pop quizzes, but you need to make sure you grasp each concept and the activities laid out before moving on to the next one. Don't skip ahead. I see you—pun very much intentionally intended!

PART 1

Self-Love

CHAPTER 1

You Can Run, but You Can't Hide

"The use of love is to heal. When it flows without effort from the depths of the self, love creates health."

–Deepak Chopra

One of the most fundamental basics we like to cover here at Energy U is making sure you understand expectations. Let's go over what happens when you're sick and can't make the curriculum provided here. You see (pun intended), it's ready for you to absorb, but it comes with a caveat. Don't push yourself when your body is telling you to stop. Energy U abides by this policy: If you're sick, don't come.

Let me elaborate. I want you to think back to the last time you were ill. What did you have on your plate at that time? Were you doing too much? Were you pushing through a hard season and not giving your body the rest that it deserves? I'm not a mind reader, but chances are, you were most likely pushing yourself past your limits and not taking time for yourself. What may have started as a sniffle due to too many late nights working over your laptop turned into the full-blown flu because you didn't recognize the stress you were putting yourself through.

You missed the signal, the stop sign, the "don't pass go" that your body was whispering to you, and you only obeyed when that signal turned into a full-on yell (a.k.a. when you attracted the full-blown illness). The signal usually is a feeling of fatigue, overwhelm, discomfort, or anxiety about the future. When we don't stop and pay attention, that signal signals other signals and soon, we are signaling to our body that we won't listen. When the body doesn't feel like it's heard, it starts yelling to make sure we hear it.

You now understand that our bodies are full of signs signaling to us to slow down, rest, and let go when we are going too fast, are overtired, and are trying to control every situation. When we slow down and pay attention to these signs, our bodies don't have to scream as loud. That yelling turns into a whisper, and it's no secret that when we listen to the whisper, we also feel calmer mentally. Don't let your body raise its voice to make you pay attention.

The blinking red light

As your professor, I know that storytelling is a way to get you to remember the lesson, and, friend, do I have a story for you! Let me take you back in time, to the early 2000s, which was the infancy of the technology craze. BlackBerrys were all the rage, and people lived through chats on a messaging system called BBM (BlackBerry Messenger). Back in these days (when I walked barefoot uphill, both ways, in the snow), we were lucky to have text messaging on our phone without tapping out every single letter of every single word using the numbers on our keypad.

The day that I received a beautiful shiny red BlackBerry with BBM (which is what all the cool kids were doing), complete with a keyboard with full home row keys, I felt like the bossiest boss lady there ever was. I was a young twenty-something professional living and working in downtown Chicago and was given this phone through the job I had at a start-up advertising agency.

This start-up was growing at a rapid pace, and as one of the first employees in Chicago, I felt a huge responsibility to constantly give my best, day in and day out. This BlackBerry was going to change my life. I would be able to write an email at any time, anywhere! I could look professional on the L train commute to work, using my home row keys on my tiny BlackBerry keyboard as a distraction tool to avoid looking into the eyeballs of strangers. I could pull out my BlackBerry in a meeting to check my calendar and see if I was busy or available to take the next meeting. I loved sending an email anywhere, anytime I wanted. I loved the ability to have technology at my fingertips.

I was so excited to have this new piece of technology in my hand. I had waited forever to get BBM, to type an email on my phone, to walk down the street with this device that signaled "I am a professional." I felt so cool. I felt so #boss.

I was living this #boss dream and riding the technology wave for the first few weeks after receiving this magical device, until it dawned on me: My boss could reach me anytime, anywhere he wanted. I was obligated to respond because the phone was owned and paid for by the company. What felt like pure technology bliss now felt like a handheld prison as I realized I was tethered to the phone and to my job 24/7.

To round this out, at the top of the BlackBerry, there was a little red light that blinked when you received an email or notification. For whatever reason, I did not know how to turn off this light. Perhaps I didn't look hard enough, perhaps I wasn't technologically savvy enough, but the light was constantly blinking on my phone, and I could not make it disappear.

Because of my type A tendencies, I would respond to every email in my inbox by the end of every day. After feeling very accomplished, I would then put my phone down, ready to release the job duties and responsibilities and move on to my personal life. I found great satisfaction when the blinking red light disappeared. But, never fail, no more than a few minutes later, a new email would come in, and the light would alert me that something else needed my attention.

This blinking red light became my kryptonite. I would see the light, pick up the phone, and respond to whoever and whatever. I would do this at all hours, on nights and weekends, as my job swiftly started to become my life. There was no escaping it. I saw senior leaders in the organization respond to emails instantaneously, and I thought that was what I needed to do to thrive and grow.

On one Saturday evening, which just so happened to be Halloween, my boyfriend (now husband) and I had big plans of going to a Halloween party. I was going to be Amy Winehouse. I had the perfect wig, a set of fake tattoos, and phony cigarettes. As I got ready, the light on my BlackBerry kept winking at me, glaring red like a giant zit smack dab in the middle of my forehead. I decided to not look at my emails, afraid of what I would receive on a Saturday.

As I drew on some smokey black eyeliner, my BlackBerry started ringing. At this point, I had fake tattoo sleeves up and down both arms, had smudged my smokey cat eyes for the full "lead singer in a band" effect, and was just about to slip on my ginormous Amy

Winehouse wig. As I picked up my BlackBerry, I realized that it was my boss.

"Have you not been checking your emails?" he asked.

"It's a Saturday," I responded. We had teams all over the country working over weekends, but my schedule was Monday through Friday, nine to whenever I stopped working (which was usually midnight). I should not have been surprised by this question, but in this instance, I was.

"One of your market managers got into an altercation at the event site," he said. "We need you to get a flight to Los Angeles and back tomorrow to let him go."

I sat there in my fishnet stockings, short jean shorts, and tank top, covered in heart-and-arrow "mom" tattoos, stunned. There was no way of getting around this. I had to jump on a plane in less than twelve hours and come back home that same day. I also had to let go a great employee, on a Sunday, and then was expected to go into work on Monday morning.

My Blackberry dreams were ruined, as was my makeup, now dripping down my face from tears. This was the icing on a very dry cake that I had let sit out for too long. My job was affecting my life and my mental and physical health. I could not escape this blinking red light—no matter where I went or what I did. In theory, red lights usually mean stop, and I knew that this was what I needed to do. *Would* I do it was the real question.

Are you running to or away from something?

Spoiler alert: Instead of stopping, calling it quits, and leaving this job, I decided to run. I decided to run 26.2 miles, in fact. Yep, a full marathon. I had been slowly training for half marathons and knew that a marathon was something I wanted to check off my bucket list. I also knew that running allowed me to leave the BlackBerry at home and escape into my iPod for an hour each day.

This was the early 2000s, and technology was not in a place where we had music on our phones, so the BlackBerry would have a forced pause for one to two hours in the evenings while I trained. It ended up being the only time of day I felt free. Sometimes the training called for longer time periods, so I would be off my phone for up to three hours. I didn't have children or pets, so my excuse when I couldn't be reached outside of work was that "I was running."

During this tumultuous period of my career, I leaned on my dad for support. He is my greatest advisor when it comes to business, and I very much value his opinion. He would ask, "Are you running *to* or *away* from something?"

In this case, I was 100 percent running away. Sure, I wanted to run a marathon and accomplish a goal, but deep down, I knew I was running from the BlackBerry-tethered blinking red light and the need to be always available and on. I was racing away from the need to drop what I was doing at a moment's notice in my personal life and be at my job's beck and call.

Now, you're probably thinking, *Why in the world would you choose to run a marathon?* As a type A overachiever, this was the *one* thing I could put my own energy into, and it was mine. It was not someone else's goal or expectation, it was my own, and truthfully, at the time, it was my only escape. So I put *all* my energy outside of work into it. I got the best running shoes, followed the Hal Higdon training schedule to the minute, and ran as far as I could *away* from work.

I trained and ran the race with two of my childhood best friends. The day of the race, 10/10/2010 to be exact, was an absolute whirlwind. All was going to plan until mile fifteen, where I tripped and fell flat on my face. My knee started bleeding immediately; my hands had raspberries on them. After the initial impact, I got back up, wiped away the blood, got a Band-Aid at a first-aid station, and kept right on running. Five minutes later, a very attractive senior leader in my organization who had also tried to escape work by training for this race came running up next to me.

"Erin, good job!" he said. Rather than chiding me for falling down, I assume he meant he was impressed that I got back up.

"Thank you!" I muttered, waving a bruised and battered hand and nursing a throbbing knee as he sped right past me.

Next to childbirth, miles twenty through twenty-six were the most painful thing I've ever encountered. I wanted to stop so many times. I cried the entire last six miles. On mile twenty-five, I said to my childhood besties, "I have to walk."

My dear friend Missy looked me in the eye, grabbed my hand, and said, "You can walk the rest of your life. Run one more mile."

My two dear friends and I ran the last mile of the race together. We crossed the finish line, all three of us holding hands in victory, shock, and severe pain.

The marathon happened on a Sunday. On top of falling and hurting my knee and hands, I also lost a toenail. I was quite the sight, but because I feared losing my job and wanted to perform, I went to work that very next day. The senior leader who saw me hobbling along had taken the day off.

I showed up and wore my invisible medal with pride. No one cared that I had run the longest race of my life the day before. They needed (wo)manpower and hands to help with client deliverables. I pushed through that day, as I did many days.

Not long after that, I came to work with a 104-degree temperature. Another day, I worked from home when I was sick with the flu and could barely move because a client deck was due. I worked through a stomach virus during a weeklong activation in Minneapolis.

I gave everything to this company. I learned so much in the process and made some lifelong friends, but the job gave me so much stress and anxiety. I was depleted, burned out, and at an all-time low. I knew I couldn't keep running away. I needed to face my fears head on and run *toward* something. If I didn't start running toward a new future, instead of away from my present, my body was going to shut down and force me to stop.

Your body sends signals

The word *disease* means exactly what it sounds like: *dis-ease*. *Dis* meaning without, so without *ease*. When you are overtired, overworked, and overwhelmed, your body tells you to slow down. This can come in the form of the common cold, a cough, or some type of physical pain. If you listen to these signals, you can prevent chronic anxiety, burnout, or in my case, running 26.2 miles. If you don't listen, your body will find a way to catch up with you, which could lead to chronic pain. Stress and anger are usually the underlying emotions that cause disease and illness.

In the book *When the Body Says No*, doctor and author Gabor Maté identifies three factors that universally lead to stress: uncertainty, the lack of information, and the loss of control. All three of these are present in the lives of individuals with chronic illness. He goes on to state that "many people may have the illusion that they are in control, only to find later that forces unknown to them were driving their decisions and behaviors for many, many years." By repressing and dissociating from our emotions, we run the risk of illness.

Specifically, Maté goes on to say, "Those who repress emotions are more at risk for disease. Repression, the inability to say no, and a lack of awareness of one's anger make it much more likely a person will find herself in situations where her emotions are unexpressed." When you repress your own feelings, put others' needs in front of your own, and dissociate yourself from your emotions by throwing yourself into work, it's as if you are opening your arms to embrace discomfort and pain.

Instead of giving this uneasiness a hug, what if you embraced yourself? What if you put your own needs first so that you could show up for your team, clients, and partners in the most productive way possible, as the truest, most authentic version of yourself, because you've taken the time to listen to your body and given it what it needs? What better signal?

Instead of a blinking red light, you are green-lit to go forward in a way that moves the needle for yourself personally and professionally. When you listen to your body and put time, care, and effort into yourself, you can ride the highway of dreams that you didn't even know existed—all because you listened to the signals.

Solo activity: Yes to you!

Step 1: Grab a sheet of paper and draw two lines in the middle so that it creates three columns.

Step 2: In the left column, write down the title *Ailment*. Underneath this title, list all the times you have been sick during the past year. This could be a cold, a virus, a pain in your body. List them all down in chronological order. Example: cold, virus, COVID, shoulder pain, sore throat, etc.

Step 3: In the middle column, write down the title *Activity*. Next to each ailment, I want you to write down what was going on in your life at that time. For example: cold = hosting a group of fourteen people, virus = traveling for work.

Step 4: In the right-hand column, write down the title *Self-care*. This is the most important column. In this column, you are going to write what you did for self-care during this time. Example: For the ailment of having a cold, caused by your activity of hosting that group, you could put "take a bubble bath" if you did this during that time. Or for the ailment of virus, with the activity of traveling for work, you could put "took naps during the day." If you did not do anything to take care of yourself during that time, then leave it blank.

Activity debrief

Question 1: Did you notice any correlations between the ailment and the activity you had going on in your life?

Question 2: What did you notice about yourself when it came to self-care?

Group activity: Yes to you!

Step 1: Have the group stand in a circle, and appoint one member of the group to be the scribe and take notes.

Step 2: Going around the circle one at a time, ask each group member to fill in the blanks: "I'm feeling ___ today." Allow them to insert whatever adjective they are feeling. "And I'm going to do _____[an act of self-care] to help this feeling."

Step 3: As each member is sharing, have the scribe jot down their answers.

Step 4: After each person shares, the entire group does a fist bump in the air and yells, "Yes, you!"

Step 5: The following day, ask each team member to share whether they performed the act of self-care. You can do this

in a team meeting, via email, or via messenger (such as Slack).
Ask them how it changed the course of their day.

**Go to itserindiehl.com/resources to get your
downloadable *I See You! Guidebook*.**

You can't heal what you can't see

Both of these activities hold us accountable for showing up for ourselves. The solo activity shows us what we could have done in the
past to put energy into ourselves and understand our current state of
awareness when it comes to self-love.

The group activity allows your team members to process emotions in real time, while also creating a safe space for them to bring
their full selves to work. By humanizing the work experience and
recognizing individual emotions, it makes the team feel seen, heard,
and valued. The scribe writing down the action plan holds the team
member accountable, and the "Yes, you!" celebration at the end is
another way to affirm the team members' actions. By checking in
with the team member the following day, you are showing genuine
support, as well as empathizing with your team.

When we can recognize our emotions and process them in real
time, we can postpone ailments. We cannot heal what we cannot
see. Had I taken the time to recognize my ailments during the
BlackBerry-blinking-red-light phase of my career, I would have recognized that the activities going on in my life at the time were too
much travel, too much overtime at the office, and very limited self-
care. The period of time when I ran the marathon was the most
self-care I had given myself through my entire time at this company,
and it was the most alive I felt at the job.

Unfortunately, after running the race, I went back to overworking and overtraveling, and my body started sending signals that it needed to shut down. Because I did not listen or take time to see and figure out why I was so burned out, I found myself consistently sick and agitated.

The same holds true for your own findings from the "Yes to you" activity. When you don't take the time to understand the activities that you have going on that affect you on an emotional level, you run and dissociate from your deepest feelings, and they hide within you. The hidden emotions and lack of awareness are what manifest disease and illness. When you recognize and are aware of the activity and the lack of self-care that is causing the ailment, you can turn your future toward a more kind and loving approach to work and life.

When you are sick or ill, your mind and body cannot give the energy that you seek to expend outwardly. This leads to inner turmoil and repetition of the same patterns. When you keep letting these patterns run your life, you hide from the root cause. The prescription for this is simple: Radical self-care is the medicine that the world needs.

You can run, but you can't hide from the fact that taking care of you is the first step in becoming a selfless leader. By recognizing your own blinking red lights and running intentionally toward radical self-care, you can recognize when your body sends you the signals to slow down. When you say no to pushing yourself too hard, you say yes to radical rest.

Now, as your professor and self-proclaimed selfless leader, I want you to take a rest before moving on. You deserve some you time, and here at Energy U, our motto is "You do you, boo!" So, take a walk, nap, meditate, perform a dance to your favorite song in your kitchen, because we've got to give to *thee* before we can open our eyes and clearly *see*. See you soon!

CHAPTER 2

Burning the Candle

"Let nothing dim the light that shines from within."

—Potentially said by Maya Angelou maybe

During your time at Energy U, you are going to have to unlearn quite a few things. We are packing a lot into a short period of time. Sometimes, to cram more into our minds, we must let go of things that no longer serve us—debunk myths, get out with the old, and input the new. You get the idea. Let's start with the infamous quote showcased on every #boss page of the Internet: "Choose a job you love, and you'll never work a day in your life."

Students, pupils, confidants, and newfound friends: I encourage you to unfollow, unsubscribe, and mute yourself from this conversation. Ask yourself this: What would you be doing if money were not an option? Would it be owning a tiki hut off the coast of Hawaii? The sunshine, the sand, a commute that's as simple as a walk to the beach—it sounds like the perfect workday, right? (Except for those of you who sunburn or chafe easily.) How could work possibly feel like work when you work in paradise? It sounds too good to be true . . . because it is!

In less than twenty-four hours, your cubicle sandcastle on Hallelujah Island comes crashing down when your paradise suddenly becomes a rainy, windy mud pit due to an incoming storm. Your sense of peace turns into a puddle of despair as you try to board up the hut and rush to shelter.

The first lesson to unlearn here is that you can enjoy the work that you do, but you must realize the actual definition of work. *Work* (noun) means something that requires effort—from your muscles or your brain—for some sort of purpose. Applying effort is the exact opposite of peace and relaxation, so the word *work* actually implies that we are expending effort, to which the #bossbabe Instagram culture definition of always #lovingwork can no longer ring true.

On the flip side, this does not mean that we cannot bring love and joy to the work that we do. The more joy that we bring to our work, the more effortless and effervescent it feels. In fact, at Energy U, we want you to love the work that you do but also realize that your work comes with an off switch. To be on at your job, your work must turn off when you leave or close your laptop. When a candle stays lit for too long, it starts to flicker and eventually burns out. The same is true for you.

Candle down

Speaking of light, let me shed some on you. As your professor, I think it's important to fill you in on my backstory and how I got to this amazing place of teaching you how to shine. Before founding the company that I run outside of Energy U, *improve it!*, I was a business development consultant at a recruiting firm in downtown Chicago. I worked Monday through Friday, nine to five, performed improv three nights a week, and then spent my off nights building my side hustle. Although I loved improv and had so much excitement around building my business, I had no days off. The only time I would relax was when I would do what my husband calls "burning the candle." I would go from work to a show, to building my business until the wee hours of the evening, every day for weeks. I would do this until my mind and body could no longer go anymore. Once this happened, I would face-plant, nose to mattress, swiftly on my bed. Sometimes I would be fully clothed. This would usually happen in the evenings after an improv show, a networking event, or some type of engagement where my switch was on. This face-plant was the cue to myself and my husband that my flame had extinguished. I was burning the candle at both ends, and there was little light to give to anyone or anything, not to mention the scalded fingers.

One evening, my candle flame burned so low that I basically melted into my apartment. I was working full time at my recruiting firm, performing on a sketch comedy team, and building *improve it!*—a professional development company that uses improv comedy to train professionals to be their best selves—on the side. I had been staying up all night memorizing lines for a sketch comedy show I was performing every weekend. This heavy schedule led to headaches and dizziness, not to mention constant fatigue. I developed a sore throat that turned into a full-blown cold.

Then I found out about the *RedEye Chicago Tribune* Big Idea Awards. It was the first competition of its kind for entrepreneurs in the Chicagoland area. It was the perfect opportunity for me to put my budding business on the map, but I learned about it the day before the deadline to enter.

Improve it! had one client at the time, and no one except my boss at my recruiting firm knew I was building it on the side. The competition included getting picked by judges to enter and then a later public voting round to get into the finale.

I passed the initial round and spent several days perfecting my pitch as I continued to work on my show, my business, and my day job. I made it to the finale, which included a *Shark Tank*–style pitch and voting by the public. At this point, my entire recruiting agency knew what I was doing and came to support me at the event, as did my friends and family.

The competition started at 6:00 pm and was over by 9:00 pm. They were announcing the winners right at 8:30 pm, and I knew that I had to leave the very moment after winners were announced, because I had a performance at 10:00 pm across the city. I jumped for joy as my name was shouted into the microphone. We won! We won! It was thrilling, exciting, and my crowd of supporters was right there to cheer me on.

We celebrated the big win for five minutes, and then immediately tore down the booth and raced to the next event. My crew of friends and family took Ubers from the awards in the West Loop of Chicago to my sketch comedy show on the north side of the city. For those of you who don't know the Chicagoland area, this was about a thirty-minute drive. I made it to the show just in time to put on my wig and get into my first character. The show ended at 11:30 pm, and the same crew went out for food and drinks afterward. We were starving and had not eaten at all throughout the night.

The competition was one of the most vulnerable experiences I've ever been through. I put so much time and energy into making the pitch perfect, asking friends and family to support and vote, and getting the buy-in I needed to win the competition. The win included a celebrity mentor, an all-expenses-paid trip to Punta Cana, and a partnership with the newspaper. It was the ticket and the sign that I needed to make *improve it!* a legit business and leave my full-time job to pursue what was then my side hustle dream.

Little did I realize that I was missing all the signs that my body was sending me. It was tired, it was depleted, and it needed a break. That evening, I came home and crashed. I slept from one o'clock in the morning until one o'clock the next day. I could barely move from the exhaustion and sleep deprivation. That one day of recovery turned into several days of lying in bed, binge-watching television, and trying to get my body back to life. I had burned my candle to the ground, and I was left with a messy puddle of wax. I had ignored the signs throughout the previous weeks to slow down. It took me three full days to recover.

As your professor, I want you to recognize when your candle is about to lose its flame. For me, this process became a pattern. I would throw all of my energy into building *improve it!* and my comedy career after working a nine-hour day. I would go day after day without eating well, hydrating, or sleeping properly. My energy became Upset Me to those around me (especially in the morning), and at the time, I thought that this was the only way of surviving. I bought into the #bossbabe #hustle culture and was #grinding. I felt "busy" and "important," and my ego was at an all-time high while I built something that I knew was my life's purpose. My soul was on fire, but so was my sanity. Something had to give, or else I would be able to give to no one.

Save your light

In hindsight, this period of #hustling told me that you can do what you love and you will absolutely work a day in your life. You can still be excited about taking a break. You can still be tired, even burned out. Your light cannot stay on all the time.

Think of your favorite scented candle (hello, Anthropology Volcano, I see you!). Think of yourself as this candle. You are the light, and when the candle burns for too long, it eventually burns down to the liquid wax and snuffs out. If you don't maintain the wick, it may difficult or even impossible to light it again. Eventually, it burns all the way down to the bottom of the jar, and then it's gone. You need to limit the flame—save the light—in order to make the candle last.

I was beginning to see that my wick was becoming shorter; I was feeling more finicky and frustrated, and I was not emitting the right energy into my new business. To be the light, I had to save my light. The candle had to be blown out periodically so that there was enough wick left to illuminate the path when I needed it.

How to know when the candle is burning low

Burnout is real, and it affects many professionals, especially after a global pandemic. A study in Gallup's *Global Workplace 2021 Report* showed that workplace stress around the world reached a record high in 2020, during the coronavirus outbreaks. This study showed that 43 percent of people from over 100 countries claimed to have experienced consistent stress throughout their workdays, rising from 38 percent in 2019. To add smoke to the flame, the increase of remote work has caused employees to burn out at a rapid rate. According to Indeed's "Employee Burnout Report" by Kristy Threlkeld, "53 percent of virtual or work-from-home employees are working more hours now than they were in the office. Nearly one-third (31 percent) say they are working much more than before the pandemic."

If you are questioning whether you are experiencing burnout and burning the candle down to a nub, here are a few signals that your light needs to be blown out for a while.

- You have trouble getting to sleep and staying asleep.

- You are cynical at work and have little to no patience.

- Small tasks feel like large hurdles.

- You frequently get the Sunday scaries and fear the week ahead.

- You constantly feel anxious and on edge.

- You work longer hours than expected of you just to keep up.

- You have little to no motivation to complete daily tasks.

If you are questioning whether you're close to burning out, chances are . . . you probably are.

Solo activity: Light savers

Step 1: On a sheet of paper, make a list of all the things that you love to do. What brings you joy? Is it painting, reading, coloring, running, writing, sleeping, or walking through Home Goods?

Set a timer for five minutes, and write down as many things as you can that make you happy. Don't overthink or judge yourself; just write. Keep this list somewhere you can see it or have easy access to it. Call this your *bliss list*.

Step 2: When you feel that your candle is burning low, refer to one of the items on your bliss list, and take time to make it happen. Maybe you schedule an hour at the end of the day to paint, read, or color in an adult coloring book. Perhaps you

continued

get up earlier for a run, give yourself an extra hour or two of sleep, or get a coffee and roam the aisles of Home Goods for a decorative vase.

Whatever your light saver is, make time to do it. By taking moments of time to save your light, you will save yourself many future moments of darkness.

Group activity: Light saver day

Step 1: Explain to your team the importance of banishing burnout before it begins and why self-care is the utmost priority for the team.

Step 2: Ask your team to do the above light saver activity on their own.

Step 3: Block time on your team's calendar for a light saver day. The *improve it!* team calls this LSD for short, but go with what feels right for your human resources department. This could be a half day or a full day, depending on your bandwidth.

Step 4: At least a few days before the scheduled light saver day, schedule a team meeting for everyone to share the activity they are going to do during the event. This will hold everyone accountable and build excitement.

Step 5: Encourage the team to take a picture during their light saver day and post it to a shared folder or on a Slack channel. Celebrate each individual's choice and encourage people with shared interests to connect about their experience.

Step 6: Make light saver days a consistent practice. You can encourage one day per month or per quarter; the timing is up to you. The most important thing is that you take one for yourself consistently, because that sets the tone for the team.

Go to itserindiehl.com/resources to get your
downloadable *I See You! Guidebook.*

Rest is productive

Encouraging your team to do activities outside of work that fuel them personally, not just professionally, shows your team that you care about their physical and mental well-being. By encouraging preventative self-care techniques, rather than reacting to burn out, you are saving yourself and your team time in the long run. You are allowing the candle to keep its flame by giving it some time to cool. Burning the candle isn't the only way to be productive. It is also productive to let the wax harden and trim the wick. Restful or recuperative activities are preventative for losing our light.

If I had taken a light saver day during my time building *improve it!* and around the *RedEye* Big Ideas award, I would have most likely not suffered that three-day sleeping hangover. I would not have had to face-plant and remove myself from life but, instead, would have restored myself with rest and activities that bring me joy. I didn't need to take on so much all at once. This internal shift would be the fuel I needed to shed light onto others.

Perhaps my story made you think back to a time in your life when your own light was sputtering. During that time, did you give yourself time to recharge, or did you keep burning away? If your flame was always on, what happened? Most likely, you eventually burned your candle down to ash and had to make up for in it some way, whether it be a sleeping bender or by contracting some type of illness. What would have happened if you completed a light saver day instead?

As a leader, you are not managing people. You are managing energy. Your team is looking to you to set the tone not just for tasks and corporate culture but for self-care as well. The #hustlehard days are gone, and the #slowdown and #fillupyourcup moments of tomorrow are here to stay. Your team needs to see that you take your rest seriously and that you see it as a productive part of work and life. This new way of seeing time away differently will help your team choose loving themselves over the fear of not doing enough. In the end, it will save everyone time and energy when you have team members who show up ready and refreshed. Proper rest is the most productive task you can give yourself and your team.

In order to fully manage energy, you need to be in a headspace that allows you to think clearly and have an open mind. You cannot be tired and burned out when you are managing others' energy. How will you see the solution clearly? How will you help the person you are leading feel as if they have an answer? I want you to think of yourself as the most awesome candle, with that "big wick energy," and make sure you realize that even the most energetic of candles needs time off.

Now go schedule a light saver day. Yes, right now. Go ahead, put it in your calendar.

Now that you have your light saver day scheduled and ready, I want to encourage you to take pictures of yourself on this day and share not only with your team but with me and the community. You can find my social handles at the back of the book, and use the #LightSaverDay because you know now, as a student of Energy U, that hashtags are #boss. Just kidding; we don't subscribe to the #boss culture here, but we do subscribe to community, support, and giving you a whole lot of love for taking care of your most important asset—you!

CHAPTER 3

A Whole Latte
of Anger

"If you don't fill your own cup, people will drain you dry."

–Probably Oprah Winfrey

Remember our pal Upset U, the Tasmanian Devil who ran around in the mornings like you had hot coals under your feet, squirting toothpaste all over the counter and creating a trail of clothes, books, and paraphernalia along your path of destruction? Does this sound familiar? Perhaps this was your every morning. Perhaps this *is* your every morning. If it is, know that this is 100 percent OK, and that you are not alone. As your professor, I'm here to guide you through to the other side, where Upward U awaits. When you start the day with negative energy, it is extremely hard to reset the rest of your day. Our mornings set the tone for the day to follow, and either we can let our morning run us, or we can run our morning.

Espresso yourself

As I mentioned earlier, Upset Me was a part of my life for thirty-three years. This was a pattern I developed in high school that so graciously came with me through college and then into my professional life. Mornings were my absolute least favorite time of the day. While working at the recruiting firm in downtown Chicago, I loathed getting out of bed, commuting to work on a crowded bus, and getting into my office building by 8:30 in the morning.

To reward myself for this thirty-minute trek through the city of Chicago, I would buy myself a Starbucks coffee every single morning. Now, it doesn't take a mathematician to realize that this was an investment—not only from my bank account but in my time. The lines at Starbucks are never short, and they are always filled with people sleepily salivating for their morning cup of joe.

I would race from the bus or train station to the Starbucks at the bottom of my office building every Monday through Friday. Because Upset Me never woke up with her alarm, I was always running late, which meant the Starbucks line would make me even later. I would stand in line, impatiently waiting my turn to tell my favorite barista, "A grande latte with almond milk and hazelnut, please." (Yes, I understand how basic this sounds.) Every person ahead of me who took longer than I thought they should placing their order would receive a sigh or an unpleasant shift in my body language. However, as soon as the barista called my name, I grabbed that beautiful white cup with the name "Aaron" scribbled on the back in permanent marker with pride. As soon as that first sip of burned beans hit my lips, I would feel like I had won the lottery. I had defeated the morning rush again, successfully hit the coffee bean jackpot, and now it was time to get to work.

One morning, I happened to have a meeting with one of my favorite clients around ten o'clock. I headed into the meeting, trying my best to let go of Upset Me, and turned up the charm. As I walked in, my client, Jessie, glanced up from her desk and gave me a sly eye.

"I see you've turned your morning around," she said.

I paused for a minute, stunned. Was I being punked? Where's Ashton!? "What do you mean?" I asked.

Jessie went on to say, "I saw you in line at Starbucks this morning in your building. I have seen you there a couple of times but never want to say hello because you look so . . . angry."

I got whiplash as I gracefully picked my chin back up from the floor. I could not believe she saw me that way. I could not believe she had seen me this way multiple times! I thought the anger was only in my head. Was I showing it outwardly? How did she know how pissed I was that I had to stand in the armpit of a stranger for twenty minutes on the train and then walk in a jacket that resembles a down comforter through the frigid streets of Chicago to get to my office? Would she want to still work with me? How do I explain this? Does she have a paper bag that I can put over my head to walk out the door and never return?

To get past this awkward moment, I lied. "Oh," I said, "I had just gotten some frustrating news this morning. I didn't realize I was giving off those vibes."

I quickly changed the topic to work, but the back of my mind kept spinning. Her comment sat with me that entire day—and the next, and the next. I *was* angry in the mornings. I didn't have a reason, and I didn't know any other way than this pattern I created for myself.

Even after hearing this shocking revelation, I did nothing to break the pattern. As I turned from an employee at the recruiting firm to a business owner, I would keep this pattern and emerge into our tiny, lower-level (not to be confused with a basement) office in downtown Chicago with my shirt stained under the arms, sweat dripping down my forehead, and a full cup of coffee ready to be consumed to change me into the "leader" that I knew I could be after nine o'clock. My team could feel the stress radiating from my pores as I entered the office and knew that I wasn't going to be my best until an hour or so after arriving.

Finally, a team member said to me, "I don't know if you need to feel stressed in the mornings in order to feel productive, but I'm worried about you." That comment was the catalyst for change. That comment sat right next to Jessie's about me grumbling at Starbucks, and it created an ever-growing tower of shame and dislike toward my morning self. Something had to change, and it had to change quickly.

Pour into your cup first

During this time in my career, I was also struggling in my personal life. My husband and I were going through a long battle with infertility. We so desperately wanted to become parents and had tried almost everything to have a miracle baby. We went through three rounds of IVF treatments with no luck. Looking back, I know that it was my internal state of being that was blocking our path. The womb cannot be shaky and grow life. The womb cannot be a stressful environment and create. The same is true for any creative endeavor. You must be in a peaceful and calm mental state to produce your best, most creative work.

Because of the comments, because of the infertility and the struggles we were having, I knew that I had to change the way I started my day. I started to focus on filling my own cup first in the morning so I could pour into others'. I started putting time, effort, and energy into my own mental state so that I could show up with less stress to create a more productive and purposeful work environment.

I began exercising in the mornings instead of after work when I was so tired and depleted. I very slowly started a meditation practice. What began as five minutes of guided meditation spread to ten minutes, then fifteen. I set off on a spiritual journey and started to learn how to connect with my own inner guidance. My cup had to be filled with endorphins; I needed to feel a deep sense of inner wisdom before I could be and do everything for everyone else. Essentially, I learned how to mother and lead myself before I could mother or lead someone else. This was a lesson that I needed to learn, and I needed to learn the hard way. The universe would not give me the gift of being a mother until I took care of myself.

After three years of infertility, many a science experiment, and three years of creating shifts in the way I started my day, we welcomed a miracle baby boy in July of 2019. My morning practice changed my life and helped in the creation of another one. I know it can change yours, too.

I'll let you in on a secret: If you apply these fundamentals to your life, of taking care of yourself first, you will change the way you see the world and the way that the world sees you. It all starts with filling your own cup first.

Solo activity: Fill your cup first

Step 1: Decide what you want to do in the morning to fill your cup first. Don't like to work out first thing in the morning? Then don't do it! Perhaps you love to journal, read, meditate, or just sit in silence. Brainstorm a list of ideas, then choose one way to fill your cup in the mornings.

Step 2: Set your alarm thirty minutes earlier than you normally get up. For example, if you normally wake up at 7:00 am, set your alarm for 6:30 am.

continued

Step 3: Unless you are Oprah and can rise with the sun, you need an alarm to get out of bed. Put your alarm in the bathroom or across the room so you must physically get out of bed to turn it off. Do not put it next to you on your nightstand.

Step 4: Wake up with your alarm. Do not hit snooze!

There is science behind not hitting the snooze button. Doctors of sleep deprivation agree that hitting snooze most likely happens when we are in the REM stage of our sleep. This stage is one of the most restorative stages of sleep. Once the REM stage is interrupted, you don't return to the same stage of sleep, so those extra eight or nine minutes of snooze are not restful.

Step 5: Start your morning by doing the one thing you've decided to do to fill your cup first. Read for thirty minutes, journal, listen to your favorite podcast on a walk. Whatever that one thing is, take thirty minutes for yourself!

Step 6: Continue this pattern for thirty days. By doing this for an extended period, you will form a habit.

Step 7: If you are feeling ambitious after thirty days, set your alarm another thirty minutes earlier, so you are one hour earlier than your current morning routine wake-up call. What else can you add in to pour into your cup first? Perhaps you have started walking for thirty minutes in the mornings. Can you now add reading for an additional thirty?

Don't forget to adjust for your new morning routine by shifting your nighttime routine. If you're waking up an hour earlier, you should head to bed an hour earlier, too. That way, you'll get all the sleep you need but will still be able to take advantage of the early start.

Group activity: Yes, I A.M.

Step 1: Talk to the team about the importance of a morning routine. Tell them that by putting energy into themselves first, they will emit a greater output for others, and feel better starting their days.

Step 2: Have a team meeting and appoint one team member to be the scribe to jot down ideas.

Step 3: Ask the group to sit in a circle. Ask them to brainstorm ideas to start their mornings by giving to themselves first. The only caveat is that when each person shares an idea, they have to say "yes, and" to the previous person's idea. It does not go around the group chronologically. Anyone can share or express an idea, but they must use the words *yes, and* before doing so. For example, someone might brainstorm "exercise" as part of their morning routine. Then the next person will say, "Yes, and . . . reading." The next person will say "Yes, and . . . taking a walk." The list continues as the scribe writes down all the answers. Watch as the momentum builds within the team. The goal here is for the team to get super specific with their choices. So, instead of saying "exercise" you want them to name the specific type of exercise. "Yes, and running, swimming, biking," etc.

Step 4: After the team has brainstormed a long list of ideas, have each person pick one way to "fill their cup up" in the morning. Refer to the solo activity above and have them set their alarms thirty minutes earlier and commit to this morning practice every day for the next thirty days.

Step 5: Create a Slack channel or a shared drive for people to post pictures of themselves doing their morning routines. Cheer on each team member when they share.

Step 6: Check in with the team after thirty days with the debrief questions below.

Activity debrief

Question 1: What shifts have you seen in your day since you've changed your morning routine?

continued

Question 2: How has this affected the way that you show up for your team?

Question 3: How has this affected the way that you show up for yourself?

Question 4: What if you added an additional thirty minutes to your morning and got up an hour earlier? What would you be able to do with an extra hour each day?

Question 5: Have you been getting up with your alarm or hitting snooze? Challenge yourself to get up right with your alarm the next morning.

Go to itserindiehl.com/resources to get your downloadable *I See You! Guidebook*.

Better latte than never

These activities show your team that you, their leader, care about their mental and physical health. By showing them you care about their well-being at and outside of work, you are acting as a mentor in their daily lives. This idea of mentoring instead of constantly giving transactional tasks will change the dynamic of your team's relationship and provide everyone with an opportunity to thrive. The goal is, even if they leave your team at some point, that they have takeaway tips and tricks that can serve them for a lifetime. What a cool thing to see!

Had I started this practice years earlier in my career, I would have felt more cool, calm, and collected starting my day. I could have avoided moments in the Starbucks line where a client could have potentially seen steam coming from my ears instead of from my morning latte. Even though this practice was something that took me years to master, it has served me well in this next phase of my life. The saying is true: It's better latte than never to find and implement self-care practices that can serve you for a lifetime! So, Energy U, what are you waiting for? Just like a coffee bean, stay grounded and jump-start your day the right way. You and the people you serve will be so happy you have found this practice. Brew can do it! I know you can!

Now that you've realized that starting your day by filling your cup first allows you to show up with more intention and purpose, we are going to *yes, and* this concept a step further. You will use this morning routine to start to design your most beautiful and ideal day, so that you have a visual of how it looks and feels. This fundamentally changed my life, and I know it has the power to change yours, too. If applied regularly, it will change the way you see yourself and the world around you. I see you, Energy U! Let's get you thriving!

CHAPTER 4

IDiehl Days

"Self-love is asking yourself what you need—every day—then making sure you receive it."

—Who knows?

Imagine waking up every morning in your ideal environment. Let's say you love the ocean, so you wake up in your house across the street from the water. You look out the window, see the birds chirping, and head to your coffee machine to brew your favorite cup. From there, you step outside onto your beautiful long back porch and sip your coffee while reading a really good book. You start your day with a run in the gorgeous sunshine, take a long hot shower, and then slip into your favorite outfit: a muumuu and a pair of flip-flops.

From there, you head into your home office, your favorite place to work, where you start your workday with ease. You turn on your lights, light a scented candle, and sit down at your comfortable desk to start the day. You tackle your most creative projects in the morning and leave your meetings for the afternoon.

When the end of the day quickly hits, you close your laptop and head outside to the dock near your house to boat with your family. You spend the evening on the water, grazing off a cheeseboard and finger sandwiches and drinking a twenty-dollar bottle of sauvignon blanc. You get off the boat, head back home to get the kids to sleep, and wind down by listening to jazz music and taking a nice bubble bath.

Sounds too good to be true, right?

Energy U, this could be your destiny. Perhaps you were reading this and thinking to yourself, *This sounds miserable! I love the mountains, snow, and skiing. I don't like the water.* OK, do you, boo! Change everything in the dream sequence to mountains, snow, and skiing, and there is your iDiehl day! My plan was to get you thinking, dreaming, and seeing the way your day is set up differently and to help you see that you have the capacity to create a life you love.

Think about the life that you've always wanted. Where are you living? What do you want to see, hear, and smell around you? What will you be wearing? Get extremely clear on what you want for your personal and professional life, then you can work toward those goals. As a student at Energy U, it's time that you realize that you have choices, and it's up to you—not anyone else—to choose and manifest a life that fuels you creatively.

Whac-A-Moling my present

As I mentioned earlier, the beginning of my entrepreneurial career was rocky. I was figuring out how to lead many people at once while also learning to innovate and be the visionary behind the business I was creating. I was also trying to start a family and to be a great wife, a fantastic improviser, and a partner to our clients. Life was a constant to-do list, a never-ending compilation of tasks, and it came with a mind that kept its hamster wheel always running. I had no formal plan for how to grow the business, and instead of relying on strategy, I found myself constantly being reactive.

There was no rhythm to my life. It was choppy and inconsistent and came with a large share of ups and downs. It felt like I was living inside a game of Whac-A-Mole at the infamous Chuck E. Cheese. Right when I thought I had knocked down a problem, another one arose, and I had to whack that mole as hard as possible to make it go away. The pattern continued for the first three years of building the business. As you know, my fight or flight response was at an all-time high, it was tiresome, and it was unsustainable.

You know those people who constantly live in a state of confidence and success, where things flow naturally for them and with ease? I picture those people as being like a river, with a rock in the middle and the water just streaming around the rock with beauty and grace. My river was the exact opposite. It had boulders, rocks, and dams all over the place where the water got stuck, the flow felt dissociated, and the stream was completely blocked. What I just described was an actual metaphor for my mind. I was the boulder standing in the way of my stream of consciousness and inner wisdom (cue the chorus of Taylor Swift's "Anti-Hero").

Slam-dunking my future

Living a life and building a career where you are constantly Whac-A-Moling your way through problems without strategy or intention can only last so long before you reach burnout. As you know, I was known to burn the candle at both ends and, at the time, did not know or believe in light saver days to preserve my dwindling wick. I lived in constant chaos, not to mention I was extremely unhappy due to the harsh Chicago winters. I truly believe weather affects my mood, and for nine months of the year, my mood was inspired by gray clouds, cold air, and very little sunshine. I love being outside, and being outside in Chicago is only fun three months of the year. It is where I built my business, but it is not where I saw myself long term. I didn't thrive in this type of weather and craved warmth, flip-flops, and the ocean. I craved warmer weather, rays of sunshine, and a body of water in my peripheral view. I knew that this was my most creative environment and where I could thrive personally and professionally.

So, instead of sitting in my misery, I started planning. Instead of Whac-A-Moling my way day after day, in an environment that didn't serve my greatest good, what if I took the time to strategically manifest and visualize a different future? What would this feel like? Instead of taking aimless whacks at my problems, what if I was strategically throwing shots and scoring? To stick with the Chuck E. Cheese metaphor, what if my life was the basketball game where the net was constantly moving back and forth, but instead of missing and just throwing the ball at the hoop pointlessly, I was making baskets every single time? To quote the incredible Michael Jordan, "We miss 100 percent of the shots we don't take." That's a pretty powerful quote, right? He should be a professional basketball player or something with that wisdom.

After giving you all the metaphors and quotes I can muster, let me bring you back to where I was at the time. I knew that the life I had in cold Chicago was not working for me or my family. I craved something different, something warmer, and a place that fueled my highest, most creative self. How could I build a life that is ideal—I mean, iDiehl for me? (You know I couldn't resist that pun.) How could I create a life that doesn't make me feel stuck and that allows me to thrive both mentally and physically? So, the iDiehl day dawned.

Solo activity: Your iDiehl day

By understanding what you want from your iDiehl day, you will create an ideal schedule, structure, and environment that works in your favor. That multiplies your creativity, amplifies your ambition, and guides you to being your highest and best self, both personally and professionally. The iDiehl day worksheet will guide you through a series of questions that will ask you to dream big.

Here at Energy U, we do not play small! The goal is not to think about where you currently are but where you want to be. If you already have things exactly the way you want them, awesome! How can you amplify that awesome to be the absolute best? Sit in a quiet space with this activity. Grab your favorite pencil or pen, light that scented candle, and put on your favorite playlist. We are going to create a life that you are proud of living and one that makes you feel good every single day. You can use this as a solo activity and then have all team members discuss at your next meeting.

The iDiehl day worksheet

1. Think about your iDiehl morning. Where are you when you wake up? Who are you with? What do you smell? What do you see outside of your window?

2. What is the first thing you do after getting out of bed? This should build off your "Fill Your Cup First" exercise.

3. Where are you when you eat breakfast? What do you see? What are you eating?

4. What is the first thing you do when you start your workday?

continued

5. What does your office look like? Where is it?

6. What are you wearing to work?

7. Who are you working with?

8. What do you accomplish in the morning at work?

9. Where are you when you eat lunch? What are you having to eat? Who are you with?

10. What projects are you working on during the afternoon?

11. How do you wind down your workday?

12. Where are you when you eat dinner? Who are you with? What are you eating?

13. What do you do after dinner to relax?

14. What is your evening wind down routine before you jump into bed?

Go to itserindiehl.com/resources to get your downloadable *I See You! Guidebook*.

iDiehl day details

Let's look at what you wrote for your iDiehl day, starting with your mornings. What did you notice about where you are? It may seem strange to think about what you smell when you wake up, but scents transport us. Maybe you wake up and smell the ocean, or maybe you wake up and smell pine trees from outside your home in the mountains. What smell would serve your most creative and highest self? Remember that the morning sets the tone for the rest of our day, so this part of the iDiehl day is very important to get right.

Who you are with when you wake up is also a very important question. Perhaps you currently have roommates and are annoyed by their uncleanliness. This is blocking you creatively as you stay stuck in an environment that causes you stress. Perhaps this exercise made you realize you need to live alone. Your iDiehl day serves as the pipe dream, so dream big!

Next, let's look at your workday. Does it have the optimal flow? Take a moment to realize at what part throughout the day you are most creative. Is it in the morning? How can you schedule your mornings so that you do your most creative work first and then have meetings and analytical conversations in the later part of your day? Or if you know you are more alert in the mornings and prefer to have meetings first, schedule all of your meetings first thing and spend your afternoons on task-oriented activities.

How we dress during our iDiehl day also plays a very important role. Maybe you want to wear flip-flops and a sundress to work every day, but your current environment calls for a blazer and pants. How can you put strategic effort into finding a job that is more aligned with your core wants and wishes?

Who you are working with also plays a huge part in your happiness. What did you put down under this question? Maybe it's working with the team you have now, or perhaps you realize that your leadership would be better suited in a different area. How do you make this happen for yourself? What small gains can you include to make this happen, or how can you start planning your life so that you inch closer and closer toward these goals every day?

Paying attention to how you end your day helps you get to sleep and stay asleep faster. Let's get intentional about what you do before you end the day. Maybe it's taking a bubble bath, reading a good book, or turning off technology an hour before bed. Perhaps your iDiehl day says to mediate and wind down with a good book, but you are currently staying up late watching bad reality television. Realize what feels most aligned to you and allows you to show up the next morning as your best self. How you start and end your day affects your energy not only for yourself but for those around you. Be intentional with your time.

The Diehl iDiehl day

I am living proof that this activity can change your life. There are many variations of the iDiehl day, starting with a version that I read in 2017 in the fantastic book *The Artist's Way* by Julia Cameron. I completed this activity while living and working in Chicago. My husband and I had been living there for the past thirteen years and had grown very tired of the harsh, cold, very *long* winters. We had both spent significant time growing up in the southeast, graduating from Clemson University and getting married in Charleston, South Carolina. We loved visiting Charleston because of the warm weather, palm trees, access to the ocean, and southern charm. My parents lived two hours away, in Columbia, South Carolina, and would come meet us, and it always made for a fantastic vacation.

The first time I completed a version of this exercise, I realized that I fundamentally no longer loved living in Chicago. I realized that I worked best and felt my best when surrounded by sun, sand, and the ocean. I realized that, instead of wearing sweaters, tights, and boots to work, I wanted to wear a sundress and flip-flops. I realized that, instead of going for a walk around the block after work with my husband and dog in a coat that resembled a down comforter with a zipper (I wore the coat; the dog has his own), I preferred to be in a tank top and shorts with my toes in the sand.

When I took this version of the iDiehl day, I realized that I was surviving in my current environment, but I was not thriving. The cold, harsh Chicago winters played a huge part in my overall mental health, and I knew my husband felt the same. Due to this activity, we started planning as many trips to Charleston as possible to figure out how in the world we could create a life there. Each vacation, we became more and more energized as we both felt that living in this environment would change our lives. At the same time, we were trying to start a family and knew that this lifestyle would be iDiehl (again, that pun is very much intended) for us to raise a child.

In early March of 2020, eight months after receiving our miracle baby boy, we were in Charleston scouting condo locations with my parents for us to purchase as a rental income property together. The goal was to live part time in Chicago and part time in Charleston. The *how* of how we were going to make this all work was still in flux, but we knew that Charleston was calling us, and we needed to heed the call. We were so close to putting down an offer when the global pandemic hit and forced us to leave this idea behind. As the pandemic continued for way longer than expected and we realized that we could work virtually from anywhere, the findings from the iDiehl day came back into play.

We could live and work from Charleston and fly to where we needed to go for work. To make a long story short, we ended up buying a home and moving from Chicago to Charleston in October of 2020. I now live the iDiehl day that I dreamed of six years ago when I first did this exercise. I love waking up to palm trees and sunshine and having a quick commute to my home office, where I very much wear flip-flops and a muumuu while working from the comfort of my home. Some days, if I'm feeling fancy, I change it up with bedroom slippers or yoga pants.

I start my day with my most creative tasks first and then leave all meetings for my afternoons. In fact, I am even typing this very sentence first thing in the morning while looking outside my window to see sunshine, green grass, and palm trees. I'm wearing bedroom slippers and yoga pants and am excited to go outside after writing this for a walk in the sun. I feel grateful every single time I walk down the street and can see the ocean, and I will always believe in the power of manifesting your dreams. I am living proof that this activity can change your life, and I cannot wait to hear how it does so for you!

Attention to intention

By realizing what you want from your life and filling that life with the things that matter, you will have space to give and connect with others in a more meaningful way. This activity is also a great way to understand the motivation of your team members. It ultimately reveals the motivation behind *why* they are doing what they are doing at work. Listen as each one shares their answers, and ask yourself, *how can I give them more of what they want?* The closer each person gets to living out their iDiehl day, the more productive they will be. Not only will helping them achieve this goal change their lives, but it will also help them feel seen, heard, and as if their wants and dreams matter.

By paying attention to the intention behind your own and your team's desires, you will feel a refreshed sense of meaning and purpose. Think of the last time that you really checked in with yourself and your team to see what you both want. When was that? Chances are, it wasn't as recent as it could be. Life is short, so the time is now to make sure you are getting what you want out of it. By putting yourself in the optimal environment, around the optimal people, and with the optimal flow of your day, you will feel more fulfilled than ever before. When you give to yourself first, this spills over to everyone you encounter, and it is a win-win for everybody.

Energy U, get ready for all the application to come to life, and to finally understand what people mean when they say "peace of mind." This isn't a brain game; it's a life game, and you are about to be a full-time winner. Let's go!

CHAPTER 5

New Choice, New You

"Keep your thoughts positive because your thoughts become your words. Keep your words positive because your words become your habits. Keep your habits positive because your habits become your values. Keep your values positive because your values become your destiny."

–Definitely not Mahatma Gandhi

Energy U, you are crushing it. You are flying through this syllabus at a rapid pace, creating momentum in your own life, and changing your view of the world. It can be such a beautiful sight, right? Now that you have the structure for setting up your iDiehl day, and you are saving your light and taking ownership of your mornings, it's time to own another space. As I've mentioned, this space is the most important asset: your mind!

As you know, our minds are the most important organ in our body, and it's so important to do that mental strength training and get those reps in! Our minds can change the course of our day, week, and year. Our minds can create a peaceful existence, or they can be an alarming presence in how we go about our days. It's up to us to choose how we want to view the world, and at Energy U, you know that choice starts and ends with you.

You can choose fear

Energy U, let me boil down many years of self-help books and blogs into one phrase for you: You can choose your existence. You can choose how you handle situations and circumstances by asking yourself whether this circumstance is happening *to* you or whether it is happening *for* you. If you *choose* to be the victim, you will feel like the victim. If you *choose* to learn from experience, you will have learned a lesson.

Back in my early days of improv training, I played the victim. I'm not talking about as a character on the improv stage (most of the time, I played big, over-the-top characters, which I'm sure is shocking to no one). I'm talking about the victim on the stage of life. After my first year of significant improv training, I desperately wanted to make one of the ensemble teams at a prestigious theater in Chicago. Let's call it First Municipality. Joining this group was the only next step in my mind that would solidify me as a strong improviser and help propel me to Saturday Night Live–level fame.

The day came for the audition, and I was a bundle of nerves. I could hardly type emails at work the morning of, I barely ate lunch due to the queasiness of my stomach, and when I arrived at the theater before the audition, I was a sweaty hot mess. I spent most of the time waiting for my turn in a bathroom stall, standing in power poses, but mostly sweating profusely and dabbing my armpits with paper towels so my sweat-stained silk blouse wouldn't be the focal point of my stage time.

When my name was called to join a group of eager improvisers onstage, I gave an overly enthusiastic grin and hobbled with my now full-blown stomach pains to the back line to meet with the rest of the prospective comedy geniuses waiting their turn to do a two-person scene. Once my name was called, I stepped out with my scene partner, and . . . and . . . and . . . I wish I could recall what happened next, but I've completely repressed this memory. In fact, I don't remember those three minutes onstage at all. I walked back to my position in line, stunned. *What did I just say? What did I just do? Am I even alive right now? Quick, blow on your hand. OK, you're breathing.* I walked out of the theater and, for the first time since signing up to audition, realized that I might not make the cut.

Low and behold, two days later, I found out the cold harsh truth. I did not make the ensemble. However, I was recommended to reaudition after taking some scene work classes. Being the star pupil that I am (like you, Energy U), I signed up for a class and then auditioned for the second time.

The second time, I had way more limiting beliefs than I did the first: *Why would they want me? I'm not funny. I'm a horrible scene partner. I play too big onstage. I have horrible object work. And I have sweaty armpits! Can't I learn how to use deodorant properly? Why did Susan make it and I didn't? How can I be more like Susan onstage? Susan wore a statement necklace to her last audition. I'm going to do that this time, so they focus on the statement necklace and not my putrid pits.*

To make a long story long, I wore the statement necklace, but I did not hear the statement I was hoping for. For the second time, I was rejected from the prestigious group that was, in my mind, the absolute *only* solution to moving forward in my improv career. In my mind, there were no other theaters, no other schools of thought, no other options. This was it, and I was supposed to be a part of it. So, I signed up immediately for what would be my third and final attempt at getting into this notable program.

Here is the part of the story where I should tell you that persistence pays off, that if you try, you will succeed. If you get up and dust yourself off and try again, you will prevail, right? This time, I decided to get smart. I wore a sleeveless blouse to hide my armpit sweat. HAHA! I'll beat them at their own game because I know how this works. I'll get there right on time, so I won't have time to stand in a bathroom stall until I'm so nervous I can't breathe. I'll waltz right into the theater, with pure confidence, and march up to that stage like I'm Beyonce. My partner will be blown away by my confidence and will go with my ideas. Together, but really all me, I will lead us through a scene about wedding planning because that's what was going on in my life at the time, and I knew everything there was to know.

That third audition day came, and I marched into the theater right on time with my teal sleeveless blouse. But as soon as I stepped foot back into the chilling, far too air-conditioned confines of the theater, my march became a tiptoe. My walk to the line looked more like I was auditioning for Cinderella before she got her glass slipper instead of a Sasha Fierce backup dancer. My name was called for the two-person scene, and all my confidence was thrown out the window, as was my ability to think at all. I questioned myself, I said no to my scene partner's ideas (which shockingly did *not* include wedding planning), and I listened to the running dialogue in my head of: *Why are you auditioning for this . . . again?*

Let it be known that Tina Fey auditioned for this same prestigious program and did not get in until the third try. I am not Tina Fey. I am Erin Diehl, and I never once got into this program. Not on the first try, not on the second, and not on the third. No statement necklace or sleeveless blouse could cover the fact that, underneath the clothing, I deemed myself unworthy. I was attacking myself and my own improvisational abilities. It wasn't the outfit I was wearing; it was the coat of under armor that needed to be changed from "I'm not worthy" to "I am." Until I changed this under armor, no outfit could outwardly express to the outside world that I was ready for a bigger stage. I had chosen fear.

You can choose love

You can choose to continue to live in fear, or you can choose love. Once I decided that love was the better choice and stopped letting fear make decisions, I stepped into the driver's seat and took off down a highway that led me directly to my dream. Because I didn't get into the First Municipality program, I ended up going to another improvisational school. This theater taught a completely different form of improv, and I ended up not only getting a crash course in how this form worked but finding a work partner for life. I spent a year and a half at this other school. During this time, I met one of the funniest female improvisers in the world, Cristy Mercier. We became fast friends, and I knew she would play a part in my life somehow. At that time, I just wasn't sure exactly *how*.

After this other school of improv, I moved on to a third and final school of thought, where their philosophy on the stage was also completely different. This final school of thought taught me how to own my big, bold character choices onstage. It taught me to find my voice and how to be more confident in who I am as a player. It took me another year to go through this program, and it led me to the idea for *improve it!* I now knew my purpose was to help people take the monotony out of corporate training by making it a magical experience.

Instead of letting the prestigious school become the metaphorical door slam on my improv career, it was a door that swung wide open for me to step into new ways of performing improv comedy. I needed to learn these other methodologies to have a clear understanding of improv as an art form. I needed to know every single way it could be done so I could use it and apply it back to corporate America.

I attacked myself for a long time after I did not get into the prestigious school. I felt unworthy of standing on any stage and was in my head for a long time as a performer. As soon as I let go of fear and let in feelings of love, I clambered out of this anxiety-ridden shame hole. Instead of feeling a sense of lack, I felt a sense of abundance for the craft I was learning and the new people I was meeting. Instead of feeling lost, I had purpose and direction. Once I came up with the idea of *improve it!* that new choice of leaning into improv to help people become the highest, most true version of themselves became my mission. I saw my improv training completely differently, with a new energy and a reframed sense of purpose. I made a new choice, and ultimately, because of that choice, I am writing and teaching you here today.

You can choose again

Energy U, as you develop this newfound way of seeing the world around you with love instead of fear, you will understand that it all starts with you. The way you talk to yourself matters. When you think negative thoughts, you say negative words. When you say negative words, you make negative actions. It's really that simple. What you say to yourself and how you treat yourself matter.

Think of something unkind that you've said to yourself today. Go ahead, say it out loud.

It hurts to hear it, right? You wouldn't say those words to your best friend, would you? You may not even say those words to your worst enemy. Why are you so hard on yourself, yet you can be so supportive to others?

In writing this chapter, I've already had to redirect myself several times with my negative thoughts: *Erin, you aren't being witty enough. Gosh, you seem tired today. The coffee isn't working, girl! Will these zits on my chin ever go away? I am not getting to the point quick enough. Stop rambling.* So harsh, right?

Let's change this narrative inside our minds right now. I have an activity pulled directly from the improv stage that you can do anytime, anywhere to change your negative thought patterns. The good news is that you don't need a scene partner or a stage to make it work. The scene partner is that big, beautiful concept we've been working out this entire chapter: your mind. Let's get to it!

Solo activity: New choice!

Step 1: As you go about your day, recognize when a negative thought comes to mind.

Step 2: As soon as you catch yourself saying the negative thought, stop in your tracks. Clap (this is to get your attention) and shout the words "New choice!"

Step 3: Forgive yourself. Tell yourself, "I forgive you for having these negative thoughts." This part is crucial to moving forward.

Step 4: After you forgive yourself, replace your negative self-talk with a more kind, loving thought instead. For example, you might be going about your day and suddenly have to jump on a call with a coworker whom you don't really enjoy chatting with. Instead of loathing or saying, "Ugh, I don't want to do this," in that moment, clap, then say, "New choice!"

continued

Forgive yourself for having the negative thought toward your coworker. Then say your positive new choice. Your positive thought could be: *I'm excited to shed positivity on this coworker today. Perhaps I can add some love to her, and help her day turn around.*

Step 5: Step back and watch your energy shift, as well as the energy of those around you.

Solo activity: New choice! remix

This game can also be played to reframe larger situations that you've perceived as negative. To do this, follow the steps below:

Step 1: Grab a soft ball (like a tennis ball) that you can throw against a wall. Find a wall that you don't mind marking up. It's probably wise to not choose the most pristine white wall in your home, unless you like a grumpy spouse or roommate.

Step 2: Throw the ball against the wall, and as you do, say the negative thought that comes to mind about the situation. For example, let's say you must have a hard conversation with a person on your team, and you know the feedback will come as a shock to your team member. You could start with "I don't want to have this talk today," and throw the ball at the wall.

Step 3: Here's the most important part. As the ball comes back to you, think quickly, without judgment, of a more loving thought and say it out loud: "This conversation will improve our relationship."

Step 4: Repeat this as many times as needed to get out all negative thoughts. For example, your next thought might be "I know she is going to be upset" as you throw the ball against the wall. Once you receive the ball back, you might say, "I will make it a priority to truly listen to her response."

Step 5: Use these new choices to drive your next action.

Group activity: New choice!

Step 1: Start a team meeting where you know there are negative feelings surrounding a topic. Appoint one person to be the chief new choice officer—the CNCO. Their sole responsibility is to look for negative communication and redirect it. Explain this to the team before the meeting starts.

Step 2: Let the meeting start naturally, and if any limiting beliefs or negative conversation arises, the CNCO is to say, "New choice!" in that moment.

For example, team member Susan says something about a team member that comes across as negative. Susan could say to the group, "Chad is not pulling his weight on the project and is making a lot of mistakes."

The CNCO will then say, "New choice!"

Step 3: The person who had the negative thought will then come back with a more kind, positive, and loving thought instead and say it out loud to the group. For example, Susan's new choice could be: "Chad is doing his best on this project, and I am going to spend some extra time with him this week to ensure he understands the full scope."

Step 4: Let the energy shift and continue this pattern of the CNCO calling for new solutions for the entire meeting. See where the energy goes!

Go to itserindiehl.com/resources to get your
downloadable *I See You! Guidebook*.

New choice at work

In the solo activities, you will witness an instant energy shift. Forgiving yourself is imperative. Most of the time, we are our own worst enemy. Forgiving ourselves for that thought in the moment allows us to stop beating ourselves up and calm our inner child. Self-forgiveness is always the first step in healing negative thought patterns. You cannot forgive others or move forward without first forgiving yourself.

In the second solo activity, the new choice remix, you are creating an unlimited amount of positive momentum toward a person or problem. When you throw the ball against the wall, you are saying the problem out loud and omitting it. This is a huge accomplishment; half of the time we are fearful or have negative thoughts, we are not witnessing what the actual problem is. The ball coming back to you quickly disallows you time to judge yourself or the stiuation and forces you to quickly reach for the highest and best overarching response.

In the group activity, you are setting expectations about how you want the group's energy to be. Setting expectations is crucial for creating a safe space and an environment where people feel loved. When negative energy arises, it stifles creativity, innovation, and the flow of ideas. When you are in a group setting and a Negative Nancy enters the conversation, the entire energy of the room shifts. This activity allows you and the team to keep the conversation productive and inspiring. It also encourages team members to share ideas and allows their voices to be heard.

You have most likely been in a meeting where a Negative Nancy dominates the entire hour. This activity makes sure that the negativity is stifled and that the positive vibes are amplified. This allows people who are usually quieter in meetings to speak up, because they know that they will be met with a positive response. It is a forced activity but one that can be applied as many times as needed to group scenarios to raise the vibe.

Open a new door

Our limiting thoughts create limiting beliefs about ourselves and the world around us. We have the power to choose how we talk to ourselves and show up in the world. Let's be clear: This is not what society calls *toxic positivity*. Toxic positivity has been #cancelled on the Internet due to a lot of the #bossbabe culture cramming quotes and unrealistic expectations of how we show up online into our feeds. You can choose to see the world as cold, harsh, and unkind, or you can choose to see your world as warm, inviting, and compassionate. Choosing more kind and loving thoughts is a decision, an intentional action, and it is a more fulfilling and easier way to live.

The reality is that you are going to have bad days. You are going to have negative thoughts because you are a human being. Every human has them, and part of the lesson here at Energy U is finding ways to redirect that negative energy. The new choice activity provides a new mindset, a new framework, and a new way of seeing the world around you. When you change your mind, you change the way your body feels. You can prevent illness and disease. You can be a light and resource for others. You can give because you have given to yourself first. With a positive mindset, you are setting yourself up for opportunities and abundance instead of scarcity and lack. It's a better mindset, a better headspace to be in.

When you choose to change your own narrative by making a new choice, you choose a new beginning. That new beginning could open doors in your life that you would have never dreamed possible. It could open doors to a life beyond your wildest dreams. You could meet people and do things you never thought you would do, like start a business, write a book, step on keynote stages. You just have to be willing to change your narrative with a new choice and open a new door.

Give to thee, so you can truly see

Now that you've recognized how the tone of your inner voice reflects the tone of your outer voice and have the tool of the new choice, you've recognized the connection between your mental and physical health by saying yes to you, and you've put time on the calendar to save your light with your light saver day, you are now well on your way to filling your cup first and creating your iDiehl day. All these fundamentals give to the most important person in your life—you!

You see, you are important in so many people's lives. You are an amazing leader, daughter, son, parent, sibling, aunt, uncle, niece, nephew, and friend. You are needed in order to make this world go around. We need you at your absolute best internally to give to others externally. Without giving and loving yourself first, you will have nothing to give to anyone else. These activities are meant to be put into action, and by implementing them, you will start to see differently. It's as if you are putting on new glasses with the sharpest focus. Your optometrist would be so proud! This new vision is going to help you help others in a completely different way.

Congrats to you for finishing the first part of your syllabus here at Energy U. If at any time you feel your energy draining, come back to any chapter in part 1 of this book. You must master this section before moving on to part 2.

PART 2

Selfless
Leadership

CHAPTER 6

Oprah Changed My Life

"Joy is the most magnetic force in the universe."

–Danielle LaPorte

Ready to think fast, Energy U? Without judgment, I want you to think of a leader, mentor, or coach in your life who made a difference in your day to day. Bring to mind a leader who understood you as not only the employee or team member but as the *human being*. This should be a person who saw you for who you are— flawed and all—and helped you see that the work that you were contributing really mattered. Visualize that person in your mind. Now, ask yourself these questions: Did you want to show up for that leader day after day? Did you want to give 100 percent to that person because they gave to you? Did you feel like the highest, most true version of yourself because you were allowed to show up as you, flaws and all? Most likely, the answer to these questions is a resounding *yes*.

In healthy cultures, leaders make work not only meaningful but also fun. They put the team members' needs first before the transactional day to day of the job. They care about the human *being* instead of the human *doing*. In other words, they see you. When you feel seen, heard, and valued and have freedom to be yourself at work, you *want* to perform. When you *want* to perform, you want to show up. When you want to show up, productivity rises, and both you and the organization thrive.

My Oprah moment

From a young age, I knew that I wanted to help people and make them feel better. I didn't know exactly how this was supposed to happen, but I knew I got great joy from seeing a person smile. For a moment, I thought I would become a florist, because people are always happy when they receive flowers. But after killing many plants throughout my childhood, especially one so lovingly named Brian Austin Greenery (yes, this is a nod to *Beverly Hills 90210*'s teenage hip-hop DJ) I realized that was not the correct career path for me.

One fateful afternoon around the age of thirteen, I was home from school sick and lying on my family's flowered living-room couch. I was flipping through the channels as one did in the late '90s, when an episode of *The Oprah Winfrey Show* came on. I obviously knew who Oprah was, but I had never taken the time to watch her show. I sat up in my ratty pajama set from the dELiA*s catalog and watched in awe and excitement as Oprah connected with not only her guests but her audience in a way I'd never seen before. She made people in that room feel important, empowered, seen, and heard, and my jaw dropped with astonishment. *This is it*, I thought. *I'm going to become Oprah.*

I continued to watch the episode and sat in silence when it was over. How in the world do I . . . become Oprah? This one episode led to hundreds more, and in a world where the Internet only connected with the *bleep boop BUZZ crackle* of a phoneline modem and AOL instant messenger, I would wait patiently night after night as my computer slowly reached out to the wider webbed world so I could get my fingers on those home row keys to type in "Oprah Winfrey." I wanted to know everything about her career so I could follow suit. I wanted to know how she became the empathetic, kind, and loving individual you see on television. I wanted to know how in the world Oprah became Oprah.

Following this revelation, I went to college to pursue a media relations and communications degree at Clemson University. If they'd had a major on how to become Oprah Winfrey, I would have applied and done anything I could to get in. During college, I had internships at local radio stations and a news magazine in Atlanta. After graduation, I took as many emcee gigs as I could to get comfortable in front of crowds. I kept putting one foot in front of the other, trying to figure out how to become this amazing figure of a human being. I even moved to Chicago, her hometown, in hopes that I could feel her good vibes and that they would, through osmosis, make their way into me. Nonetheless, I persisted and persisted in this quest to no avail.

One fateful day in 2011, I was working at the advertising agency (the one with the blinking BlackBerry light) and saw that Oprah was retiring from her show and creating her own network: OWN.

(Oprah Winfrey Network—see? The woman's a genius!) She was starting a series of shows to begin the programming, and one of the shows was called *Your OWN Show*. This was a reality show for regular people, just like me, to go through a competition to eventually land ourselves a slot and a talk show on OWN.

Never in my life had I felt like I had more of a purpose. I called up my dear photographer and videographer friend and asked him to help me submit a tape. We filmed it the next week at my apartment in Chicago. It was the wackiest video, but it showcased my personality, which, as a student of Energy U, you know to be very subtle. Somehow, someway, my video made it through the first round of the competition! I was going to be featured on the OWN website, where the public voted to get contestants into the second round.

I was hot to step onto the campaign trail and started emailing, posting on Facebook, and sending the voting link to every person I knew. I sent it to coworkers, former coworkers, anyone from those emcee gigs. There was no Instagram at the time, or I would have blasted it there. I sent it to family members, old teachers, distant cousins, anyone with a finger who could hit "vote" on their computers. After several weeks of begging people to vote, the results came in. I did not make it into the second round.

As you can imagine, I was devastated. My dreams were crushed, and I felt as if there was nothing else left for me. This was it. This was the mountain peak, and it was all downhill from here.

That is, until one glorious day when I got a phone call from Oprah herself. She had seen my video and wanted to meet in person!

Just kidding! Wouldn't that be a story for a book? Just wait for book number two. (A girl can dream, right?!)

I did not meet Oprah, but the next best thing happened. I met Oprah's long lost soul sister.

My video had circulated its way back to the staffing agency I had done some temping at in between emcee gigs before I started at the ad firm. Yes, I was a temp at a temp agency! The branch manager was looking for a business development associate, and she thought, based off my Oprah video, that I would be great at it. I spoke with the branch manager, Jen D'Angelo, over the phone. She was so kind, so warm, so passionate about her work and about hiring me. I felt flattered, floored, and so happy to get relief from my job with the BlackBerry blinking red light.

I didn't get the talk show or experience with OWN, but during our first phone call, I knew that I had found a real-life Oprah in Jen (as opposed to the mythical ideal of actual Oprah). She was kind, empathetic, and really cared about my well-being and overall happiness. She saw me for me, the human *being*, rather than the human *doing* the work.

I had approximately two phone interviews with Jen and was then hired on the spot. Jen never met me in person but somehow knew I was the person they were looking for in this role. She knew I had never done any type of sales role before but was willing to train me because she saw potential. I accepted her offer, put in my two weeks at the BlackBerry blinking red light agency, purchased a lot of business pants from Goodwill, and started the position two weeks later.

Even though I did not win the Oprah *Your OWN Show* competition, I won something better: a new position at a company where I was valued and my time outside of work was honored, and a mentor who saw me for who I was and who I was meant to be. As far as I was concerned, I had won. I was Oprah—well, as close as I'll ever get. If I were Tom Cruise, I would have jumped up and down on a couch; instead, I jumped on a bus and headed down the busy streets of Chicago to a new life and a new leader. This was my Oprah moment, and I was here for it all.

"You get a car!"

Jen knew that I was new to the business development world, as well as the recruiting industry, and guided me each day to learn something new. She showed me through her own actions how to connect with others, how to establish trust, and how to bring your full self to work. You are going to learn so much more about Jen and her leadership in the next few chapters, because she really is a case study for how we must put energy into ourselves first in order to show up and become a selfless leader for others.

Because Jen showed up for herself, she showed up for her team. Because she showed up for our team, I, like the rest of the team, felt invested in our work and wanted to perform. I wanted to give my best to this leader who believed in me. I wanted to make her proud and do my best at every task and assignment given. I shared ideas, innovated solutions to outstanding problems, and felt like my opinion mattered because my ideas were heard. I felt valued and like I truly belonged.

This input created a different output. Because I was taken care of in my own hopes and desires, I was able to give more to our clients. I was able to show up for them and their needs because my needs were taken care of. I stayed at this staffing firm for five years because of Jen's leadership. I stayed because she believed in me and believed in my dream of building *improve it!*

Her leadership affected me on such a deep level that it has inspired the way that I lead and show up for my own team. The ripple effect of great leadership is beautiful. When one great leader creates a splash, the ripple continues with each team member. A team member can create their own splash and create lasting ripples within their teams. The cycle can continue with splash after splash, ripple after ripple—*if* we are shown the example.

The energy that we give to ourselves, the self-love that we provide to ourselves internally, affects our output externally. Jen could have never shown me that type of selfless leadership if she did not give to herself first. Because the energy she gave to me and the team was a constant display of selfless leadership, we wanted to show up for her. Because we wanted to show up for her, we were productive in serving our clients. Because we were service driven, our staffing firm started to thrive. Because we started to thrive as a firm, we started to thrive personally. It was a win-win across the board.

Think of the infamous Oprah moment where she is pointing out to her audience, shouting, "You get a car! You get a car! You get a car!" When leaders lead with a selfless mindset, everyone gets a car, because everyone feels the love. To be clear, you might not get an actual car. The car is a metaphor. But you'll get support, inspiration, and success.

Your Oprah moment

Now that you are aware that self-love and putting energy into yourself is the first step in selfless leadership, the goal is to connect this energy to your team and put all the goodness that you have amassed to good use. When we go inward, we expel good energy outward, and when we give outwardly, people inwardly feel connected to themselves and the work that they are here to do.

The next two activities are meant to be completed individually and then as a group. If you lead a team, make sure to do the group activity so you can feel the instant connection of self-love to selfless leadership.

Solo activity: Oprah's (and your) favorite things

Step 1: Using a timer, set the clock for ten minutes. Grab a sheet of paper and a pen, and write a list of your favorite

continued

things about your job. Example: my coworkers, working from home in bedroom slippers, the flexibility, the memes on our Slack channel.

Step 2: After ten minutes, review your list. Go through each item and say "thank you."

Step 3: Allow this list of your favorite things to sink in and change your vibe. Really appreciate the things that you like about where you work and the people you work with.

Step 4: Store this list in a place that you can easily come back to. This could be in your planner, a calendar, or next to your desk. One idea is to take a picture of the list and create a folder on your phone called *Favorite Things*. I like to make these lists at the beginning of every year and store them in this folder. It's fun to reflect year over year and see what things have changed and what things have stayed the same. Then, when you are having an off day, pull out the list and review it to instantly change your mood.

Group activity: Your team's favorite things

Step 1: Arrange a meeting specifically for this activity, or use it as an icebreaker at the start of a preplanned meeting. This is a great tool to use if your team is experiencing negativity of any kind. At the start of this meeting, explain that you are going to do an activity to change the vibe of each individual and raise the vibration of the team collectively.

Step 2: Start this activity by looking to someone on the team and sharing your favorite thing about them. Pro tip: Start with your most extroverted team member first to get them on board. Example: You look to Susan (who you know will take this activity and run with it) and say, "Susan, I love the way that you hold space for others when they are having a hard day."

Step 3: The person you called upon is going to say "thank you" for this compliment and choose another team member. They will then tell another team member their favorite thing about them. Example: Susan says "thank you" for the compliment, and then tells Nate on your team her favorite thing about him.

Step 4: Continue this pattern until every person on the team has had a turn.

Step 5: Step back and observe the vibration of the room now. Ask the team how they feel now that they've been seen and recognized by their team.

Step 6: Come back to this activity when you are feeling negative energy among your team members. It is an instant mood booster, and it will foster immediate connection and set a new tone for the day.

Go to itserindiehl.com/resources to get your downloadable *I See You! Guidebook.*

Your focus becomes *the* focus

When you start to focus on the things that are going well instead of the things that are going wrong, you are attracting more abundance into your work and into your life. Perhaps you are in a job that you don't really like and have considered leaving. The solo activity is great to do, especially to help you find appreciation for where you are right now. This appreciation helps you to see your current situation differently.

Do you know those moments where things start to really pick up momentum? Where one good thing happens, and then another, and then another? This is most likely because you have put yourself in a mindset to see differently and in a more positive light. When you see the good instead of the bad, you are attracting better things into your life. Just like the ripple of good leadership, the ripple of a positive mindset affects everything that you do.

The same holds true when you go in the opposite direction and focus on what you don't like or what you lack. When this happens, you are living in a scarcity mindset. There is never enough, and you don't see what you currently have in front of you. Therefore, it is hard to attract new jobs, people, and things into your life. When you focus on abundance instead of scarcity, you open the door to new possibilities, new people, and new opportunities that you could never have imagined.

The same holds true for the group activity above. Perhaps you feel the team's energy and connection flagging. Your focus has been on what is not working, how communication is lacking, and how morale is low. When you focus on what is working, what people truly enjoy about working together and about each other, you start to see things from a different perspective. This energetic shift allows the team to see differently, which brings forth new energy and momentum.

What you focus on will become *the* focus, and if you focus on negative energy and situations, you will bring more of this into your day to day.

It's a lot to take in, I know. But you are crushing it, and making me, Oprah, and hopefully *yourself* proud. Is it safe to say your vision is changing and things are starting to become more clear and in focus? I know you're seeing differently, and we've got more vision tests to ace coming your way. Let's go!

CHAPTER 7

Eight, Nine, Jen

"I want to be around people that do things. I don't want to be around people anymore that judge or talk about what people do. I want to be around people that dream and support and do things."

–Amy Poehler, according to QuoteQuoter.com

The time has now come for your first real vision test. Go ahead and close your eyes. Seems counterintuitive, right!? I know you think this is silly, because you need those eyeballs to read this book, but bear with me. With your eyes closed, I want you to think of a mentor, boss, or coach who changed your life. Go ahead and give them a solid few minutes of envisioning their presence in your life.

What words come to mind when you picture their presence? Empathetic? Kind? Loving? Compassionate? How did that person carry themselves? Did they show up with negative energy first thing in the morning like Upset U? Or did they put energy into themselves first so they could show up in a more meaningful way like Upward U? Did they call you at all hours of the day when you weren't at work, or did they set clear boundaries with your personal and professional life?

Chances are, this person was a selfless leader, someone you would like to emulate in your own leadership style. These leaders are gems, needles in haystacks; many leaders do not understand that the connection that they have with themselves is what helps them show up as a selfless leader for their team. We need to celebrate these rare breeds, cherish them, and study their actions so we can bring more selfless leaders to the world. I personally know one of these precious jewels, and this shiny, amazing human happens to be my former boss, a person you are now familiar with, as she gave me my first and only Oprah moment.

You're a "Jen"

Jen D'Angelo is the best boss I've ever had and ever will have. (As an entrepreneur, it is my goal to never have a boss again, although I do feel that my toddler fits this bill at various times.) She was a single mother and the epitome of a cool mom. Jen lived an hour and a half from our recruiting firm in downtown Chicago. She would make this trek to our office every morning from the suburbs of Chicago, park, and enter the office filled with Reese Witherspoon–like sunshine. There was no trace of negativity or any sign she had just spent an hour and a half of her morning in bumper-to-bumper traffic and exhaust fumes.

As she entered the building, she greeted every single person with a smile and a "how are you?" and then would ease into the day's work. She would spend her mornings brainstorming or working with clients or a team member who needed coaching. When lunch rolled around, Jen would encourage us all to get away from our computer screens and take breaks. We had a gym in our office building, and she encouraged us all to join and work out during the full hour break that we were obligated "by law" to take, as she would joke. Because of her intentionality in prioritizing physical and mental health, I joined her at the gym almost every day. She set very healthy boundaries for her work hours and would leave around four o'clock on most days to go pick up her son. This was her typical day and week, and she did it with grace.

However, there are no typical days working for Jen D'Angelo. Jen loved to have fun, and it spilled over into every facet of her job. Both she and I were responsible for the business development of the firm, so this meant a lot of lunches, in-person client meetings, and after-work networking events. Jen loved to make them fun and interesting.

In my first month at the job, we decided to go to our clients' offices on St. Patrick's Day. We purchased lots of St. Patrick's Day flair, including big green hats, green feathered boas, and huge shamrock sunglasses. We bought tons of chocolate gold coins and carried them with us as we walked into corporate office buildings looking like we were heading into O'Brien's Pub for a St. Patty's Day celebration. The clients would greet us in their lobby, and because they had such well-established relationships with Jen, they would start crying from laughter. Jen would encourage me to do wacky dance moves in the lobby of said offices, and of course, I would oblige.

On Halloween, we dressed up in witches' costumes, made custom root beer labels that said, "Enjoy Your Brew," and hand delivered them to clients. Again, our clients savored the creativity and the audacity behind this intentional gift.

On Friday afternoons, the security guards in our building would laugh hysterically when half our office would come rushing into our building with cases of real beer, wine, and many bags of chips from the Walgreens across the street to start our four o'clock Friday happy hour.

Jen loved pranks, and so did our office. We pranked everyone from each other to our partners and spouses, and even the manager of that gym downstairs. Jen loved celebrations, so she made sure that every single person was celebrated on their anniversary and birthday. We had birthday plates and napkins in bulk in our office kitchen, because there was always someone or something to celebrate.

For my thirtieth birthday, Jen even had my best friend, Betsy, help in the surprise. Betsy knew and loved Jen, and Jen asked her to make me late the morning of my birthday, so they could decorate. When I got to work, the entire office was saturated in embarrassing photos of me, and they had planned an afternoon dance party to celebrate. My wedding shower was also a surprise and was elegantly thrown in our office conference room, with my favorite sushi and champagne. On my last day at the staffing firm, Jen and the team created a scavenger hunt and they had me wear a GoPro to my favorite locations all around our office building to film.

You may think that this was just my experience, that Jen played favorites or went out of her way especially for me. This is not the case. Every single team member felt this love. We were a small office of nine women, and every single one of us was celebrated when it came to our birthday, anniversary, or a special event in our life. No expense was spared to make us feel seen and that we truly belonged.

Be the Jen you want to see in the world

Can you imagine if every person in the world was led by a leader like Jen? What would work feel like? How would you feel daily? What would our world feel like? As you can imagine, it would be a much more inclusive, exciting, and fun place, where everyone could see their highest potential because that potential was reflected back to you. When a leader truly sees you, you feel as if you can accomplish anything.

Jen was intentional in how she showed up to work every single day. She made her life outside of work a priority. She focused on her mental and physical strength by exercising and thrived on eating healthy foods. She regularly took time for self-care and encouraged all of us to fill our kettles first. By putting this time and energy into herself first, she showed us how to give more love to ourselves. Because she was intentional about putting time, effort, and energy into herself, she was able to fully give to others.

Let's now take a deep dive into your own energetic levels and the way that you show up in the world. These activities will encourage you to truly examine your leadership abilities where you are right now.

Solo activity: Give it a 10!

Step 1: Think about the energy you want to bring to work every day. Define what low energy means for you. Example: Low energy may mean feeling lethargic, foggy, and slower than usual. Write your answer down at the top of a sheet of paper.

Step 2: Define what average energy means for you. This is your baseline. How would you define the energy that you show up with consistently? Example: Average energy means I am rested, calm, and in control of my day. Write your answer down.

Step 3: Define what high energy means for you. This is your optimal energy, and the energy that you are striving for. Example: High energy means you are showing up rested, with clear and sharp focus, and can listen empathetically and think quickly on your feet. Again, write your answer down.

continued

Step 4: Now write down your overall energetic score for the day. Take an estimated guess as to the average score on a 1–10 scale.

Step 5: Now draw lines to divide the rest of your page into three columns. Create a list of people you had one-on-one conversations with throughout the workday in column 1. It does not have to be a comprehensive list but list the people whose conversation stuck out to you.

Step 6: In column 2, write down the energy level of the conversations you had with each individual, on a 1–10 scale based on the energy you received from the other person.

Example: Let's say you have a conversation with Susan from accounting. She is having an off day because, over the weekend, she gave all her time and energy to helping a friend move. Susan is mopey, tired, and barely able to stay awake for your conversation. Rate Susan's conversation as 1.

Step 7: In column 3, rate *your* energy levels after conversing with this person. This can differ from your daily average at the top of the page.

Example: Let's say you gave yourself a 5 (average energy level) for the day. In column 2, you rated your conversation with Susan as a 1. Susan's energy affected yours and brought you down from a 5 to a 1. In column 3, you would write a 1, even though your energy for the day was a 5.

Step 8: Take a moment to reflect on the numbers you see in both columns 2 and 3. Is there a correlation between the energy of the person you encountered (column 2) and your own energetic level (column 3)?

In the above example, did Susan's energetic score of 1 cause you to have an energetic score of 1, or did you stay at your baseline energetic score of 5? The opposite could also be true, where you are speaking with someone and they increase your energy levels. Take some time to reflect on these answers and notice any correlations.

Group activity: Make it a 10!

This activity works best if completed in person with enough space for the team to walk around.

Step 1: Tell the team that you are going to do an activity to demonstrate energetic levels at work.

Step 2: Before explaining the activity, ask your participants to hold up a number—1, 5, or 10—with their hands and to place their hands on their forehead. Do this on the count of three, so people don't have time to judge themselves.

Step 3: Instruct your participants that if they held up the number 1, they are now low, negative energy. If they held up the number 5, they are now average, mid-level energy, and if they held up the number 10, they are now high, positive energy. Tell them they will now embody energy at that level when you say go.

Step 4: Ask your participants to walk around the space. Instruct the group that you are going to say "partner," and when you do, they are going to find a partner and start having a conversation about their upcoming weekend plans. The goal is that they will have this conversation using their designated energetic levels.

Example: If two people partner and one is a 10, that person will go about the conversation using high energy. If the other partner is holding up a 1, they would have the conversation using low energy.

Step 5: Let the conversations continue for one to two minutes with the first sets of partners, and then yell "partner" again. Have them change partners a total of three times so they have an opportunity to connect with three different people, and

continued

then gather the participants so you can ask them the following debriefing questions.

Activity debrief

Question 1: What did you notice about your own energetic levels as you were communicating with others?

Question 2: Did your own energetic levels start to shift as the result of the other person's energy? For example, if you were a 10 but having a conversation with a 1, did your energy start to become lower?

Question 3: What does this activity show you about how energy is mirrored back to us?

Question 4: In situations where you feel like you might be receiving low, negative energy, how can you respond with positive energy to raise the frequency of the conversation?

Go to itserindiehl.com/resources to get your
downloadable *I See You! Guidebook*.

You are responsible for you

What both energetic activities teach us is that you are responsible for your own energetic levels. Let's say you start the day with high, positive energy but work alongside someone with low, negative energy. It is up to you to protect your own energetic boundaries and not allow their negative energy to bring you down. You are responsible for keeping your energetic levels where you want them. You can change how you feel around energy vampires, people who suck the energy out of you.

The opposite is also true. If you emit negative, low energy in conversation, you are responsible for changing your mindset to get to a higher energetic level. The person you are conversing with is not responsible for raising your energetic levels, and you should never try to bring someone down with you.

The energy you give outwardly directly correlates to the energy that you receive back. If you emit negative energy, do not expect positive energy in return. If you are giving positive energy to others, chances are, you will receive that energy back. If you don't, perhaps you limit your time with the people who bring you down. Our mindset and energy are ours to control, and we, not others, are in control of how we want to use it to show up in the world.

If you are cognizant of your own energy levels before a meeting or conversation with your team, you will emit energy more consciously and get a different return from your team members. If you are unaware of how you are showing up, try to become more conscious. The closer you get to consistently providing level-ten energy, the more positive energy you will receive in return. This creates a domino effect of positivity, which helps everyone enjoy their environment that much more.

Now, as your professor, I sense some hesitation from you. You're asking me to think about the way I show up, every single day, you say? You want me to change my mid-level energy to positive energy on the regular? That sounds exhausting. You want me to give and give and give without perhaps receiving anything but negativity in return? Professor Diehl, what's the return on investment in that?

Before you quit before the semester is over, let me assure you of this, Energy U: It sounds exhausting because it is. Positivity is a choice, it's intentional, and the very best leaders (like Jen) do it every single day with zero expectations of anything in return. These leaders do it because it's the right thing to do. They do it because they are choosing to be the example, and if it doesn't start with them, who will it start with?

If this is not your wheelhouse, you can start by making small changes every day. Try using *yes, and* to postpone judgment of conversations. Instead of negating a team member's idea, listen and provide feedback. Instead of scoffing at the idea of your team member taking another day off, applaud them for taking the time to rest and recharge. Small actions lead to big results, and if you intentionally focus on these small actions, you will eventually become the leader that you wish to be led by.

Leadership is not for the weak, and you, my friend, are stronger than you think. So, get in those reps of positive energy. Start building that muscle, so your team, family, and friends can bask in the energy of the positive, strong bodybuilder—I mean teambuilder—you will become.

CHAPTER 8

The Empathy Ladder

"Empathy is a quality of character that can change the world."

–Barack Obama

Have you ever truly felt empathy? Has anyone ever listened so intently, so deeply that you thought they were right beside you in your situation, walking hand in hand with you or perhaps even wearing your shoes? Thought leader and research-based qualitative psychologist Brené Brown says, "Empathy is connection. It's a ladder out of a shame hole." If we want to show up as selfless leaders, we must first understand this on a fundamental, deep level.

You've heard the saying *put yourself in their shoes*. Empathy means putting on a pair of their Nike Dunks, walking around in them, getting a blister, and then having a conversation about what the experience was like after handing the shoes back to their rightful owner. It means truly understanding where a person is coming from, not just in that moment, but in the many moments in that person's lifetime where you have not been. Understanding the full person, the full situation, the full picture. Becoming a selfless leader means applying radical empathy to any and every situation, not acting as yourself while wearing the Nike Dunks but truly embodying the feeling of the other person.

True connection to yourself and outward, selfless connection to others cannot exist without empathy. When there is a surplus of empathy, there is a surplus of trust. When empathy is lacking, so are connection, hope, confidence, and belief in the team, as well as in the leader. When you feel hopeless and unsure and don't carry a strong conviction in the mission or purpose behind the work you are doing, you desire more. You constantly start to think the grass is greener or wonder what else is out there for you. You start to really dislike going to work and constantly get what many call the "Sunday scaries." You fear the week ahead, and your mind is filled with dread about what situations you might encounter in the upcoming week.

Is this sounding all too familiar to you? Don't worry, Energy U. Everyone has had an experience with a boss or leader who does not have an empathetic bone in their body, so know that you are not alone, my friend. In fact, here is a story all about my own experience with an unempathetic leader that might hit home.

Climbing the corporate ladder

Now that you know the story of the infamously energetic, compassionate, and empathetic Jen, it's time to meet her antithesis, Chad. Chad was a leader that I had before Jen, and one who was very eager to climb the corporate ladder. He had a very determined mindset to climb this ladder quickly and swiftly and would push aside anyone or anything that stood in his way. Remember the marathon I ran to escape the blinking BlackBerry red light? That red light blinked constantly from many wishes, wants, and demands from—you guessed it—Chad. That blinking red light still haunts me to this day. It was like a constant blaring siren in my head. My flight or fight mode was in a perpetual state of arousal, and even in times when I should not have been working, such as during evenings or weekends, I would live in constant fear that my Chad siren (the blinking BlackBerry red light) would go off, and I would somehow be needed at that very moment.

As you know, I once had to fly out early on a Sunday morning in full Amy Winehouse fake tattoos and back home that same evening due to the Chad siren going off. I would go to bed and wake up with the Blackberry blinking its beady red eye in my face after receiving a series of emails from him after ten o'clock at night. Most of the emails included a to-do list for me, most of which he expected to be completed by ten o'clock that same morning. Upset Me would be in full swing, throwing things around while getting ready in my tiny apartment and then running while dripping sweat down the streets of frigid Chicago to hop on a bus and meet the Chad siren at the office for what would be a whirlwind of tasks and to-dos.

After a year and a half of dealing with the Chad siren, I finally broke. The company had a fantastic year and, as a result, was taking all team members who had been there a full year on a trip to the Bahamas. We were headed to a beautiful, all-inclusive resort, and all team members were super stoked because it was a reprieve from the constant chaos of our day-to-day work. I was thrilled and felt very privileged to be included, except for the fact that Chad expected me to work overtime to complete several client decks before we left.

The day before our trip, a few members of the team decided to use our lunch hour to get our nails done. I was excited for this luxury because I was way overdue in the self-care department. I knew I still had hours of work to do before we embarked on this journey, but the one-hour break and escape sounded lovely. As I packed up my bag and headed to the door with the rest of the team, Chad stopped me right before I made my exit.

"You're going to go too?" he asked.

"Yes," I replied.

"Don't you have a lot of work to do?" he said with a sheepish grin.

In that moment, time froze, my ears started whistling, my face turned bright red, and I dropped my belongings on the floor.

"Do you really expect me to miss out on this one-hour lunch break that I never fully take and a fun team outing to spend one extra hour working?" I asked.

He sat there, looking absolutely stunned, and replied, "Well, the client needs this by end of day."

I picked up my belongings that I had thrown down in frustration, ran to the bathroom, and sobbed. This was during my mid-twenties, before I developed a backbone. I didn't think I had a leg to stand on when it came to standing up for myself. I would love to tell you that I yelled, "Peace out, sucker!" and walked out the door like a mature, responsible twenty-something. OK, that's not the most appropriate thing to do, but it might have been better than staying.

I would love to tell you that I quit right then and there or that I asked Chad why working so hard and climbing to the top of the corporate ladder so quicky was so important to him. I'd love to say he responded with a beautiful answer, that we hugged it out and then had a proper adult conversation that ended in us both seeing each other differently and from then on, our relationship changed for the better.

The end of the story is very anticlimactic, and honestly quite regretful. I ended up skipping the spa date with my coworkers, working through my lunch break while scarfing down a stale sandwich from Jimmy John's, staying extra late at the office that evening to finish my work, rushing home to pack, and then waking up the next morning to meet my team at the airport for this awesome all-inclusive trip. I did not have priority seating or boarding, but high on my priority list was staying as far as humanly possible away from Chad.

Chad did not see me; he only saw what I could do for him. He saw me as another rung on his way up the corporate ladder, and he would climb over me to get to the top. However, there were times when I did notice that Chad saw potential in me. When he moved me off one client project to another because he needed his "star players" on this fast-moving client deliverable, I knew he valued my work.

When Chad would call or email me on the weekends, I would respond because I wanted him, as well as the team, to succeed. However, I also knew that if I didn't pick up or respond, I would be met with a "PS" conversation on Monday. This acronym stood for *professional setback*, and it was a constant conversation and joke among Chad and his senior-level peers. I would hear this on occasions when I didn't commit to afterwork happy hours with the team so I could train for the marathon or when I didn't commit to time spent outside of the office "bonding" with things like book or wine club.

As a corporate ladder climber, Chad was going at full speed, step by step, racing to the top with the fullest force—and was happy to crush anyone under his steps. During this time, I learned very quickly never to trust a ladder climber. They are always up to something. This lack of trust and empathy started to really mess with my nervous system and with my mental and physical health. I was stuck at the very bottom of this ladder, and I felt stepped on.

The empathy ladder

Because this quote is so good, and so spot-on with this conversation, let's hear that quote from Brené Brown one more time. "Empathy is connection. It's a ladder out of a shame hole." To say I was in a shame hole would be an understatement. I was inside a hole inside the shame hole, down at the bottom of the shame pit. I constantly felt humiliated, distressed, and foolish for staying at this job when I knew there was no way to continue this path mentally and physically. Although I loved my coworkers and the company, I knew working for Chad and hearing his constant siren would eventually bury me.

I needed a leader who cared less about climbing the corporate ladder and more about climbing the ladder of love, kindness, and compassion—the empathy ladder. I needed someone to see me for me, and as you know, Jen was the ten that dropped her ladder down into the hole of shame and pulled me right out. After our phone interview (and her witnessing my Oprah video) I was relieved of the Chad siren and met with a new opportunity.

With Jen as my new guide, I climbed out of the shame hole and up the ladder of empathy rung by rung. As I reached for daylight, I saw my strengths and my gifts, because Jen saw them too. Instead of feeling humiliated at work, I felt empowered in my new role. Instead of feeling distressed, Jen helped me to create balance in my personal and professional life and to do things that help me focus on my self-care instead of neglect it. Instead of feeling foolish about what I was doing with my career, I felt clever and inspired to do great work for a great leader who saw my potential.

I stayed in the job with Chad a year and a half. I stayed in the job with Jen for five years, until I decided—and she encouraged me—to build *improve it!* See the difference that empathy makes?

If you only try one activity out of this book, let it be the following one. This activity can help you be a better parent, partner, friend, and leader, with the highest level of empathy. This activity has a brilliant ah-ha-ha moment at the end—where the light bulb goes off and you are laughing at the same time—so please, try this one at work or at home.

Solo activity: Empathy

Step 1: Take out your phone or any technology that has a recording capability.

Step 2: Think of the biggest challenge you are facing right now. It could be getting a promotion, dealing with a team member, a sick family member—anything.

Step 3: Hold up your phone or recording device and prepare to hit the record button. Record yourself on camera, discussing the challenge you are facing. Let this continue for one minute or until you have completed discussing the challenge.

Step 4: This is the hardest part. Press play and listen to yourself stating the challenge. You can do this! Please note that everyone hates seeing themselves on camera, so you are not alone!

Step 5: Take yourself out of your own shoes for a minute. Go ahead; slip them off! Pretend you are a friend listening to this challenge. What advice would you give your friend? What advice would you tell your best friend based on the challenges you are facing?

continued

Group activity: Empathy

Step 1: Ask your team members to partner up. Ask the partners to sit close together, facing each other. Ask them to decide who has longer hair; this will be partner 1.

Step 2: Partner 1, who has the longer hair, will explain to partner 2 a challenge that they are currently facing at work.

Step 3: Partner 2's job will be to listen intently to partner 1 as they state their challenge. That's it—just listen.

Step 4: After partner 1 has finished discussing their challenge, partner 2 will then repeat the challenge back to partner 1 in first person. This is extremely important in completing the activity. Make sure that partner 2 is using "I" statements and repeating back to partner 1 their challenge, as if it was their own.

Step 5: The partners will then switch, and partner 2 will state a challenge to partner 1. Partner 1 will then repeat the challenge in first person.

Activity debrief

Question 1: What did it feel like listening and responding to your partner using the first person?

Question 2: What did it feel like as the partner hearing their challenge repeated to have it repeated back in first person?

Question 3: What did this activity teach you about listening?

Question 4: What did this activity teach you about empathy?

Go to itserindiehl.com/resources to get your downloadable *I See You! Guidebook*.

Feel the emotions

This exercise exemplifies empathy to its core. It recognizes that human beings truly don't take the time to feel what another person feels on a regular basis. By using the first person and repeating back exactly what your partner said, you are putting yourself in the other person's shoes. To do this, you must first listen intently, then also feel and see through the lens of your partner. Putting yourself in the first person allows you to truly embody their feelings. Feeling allows us to understand emotions on a deeper level than just listening. Empathy evokes a feeling, and that feeling can change the way we show up for others.

When we can truly empathize with our team, we are able to take ourselves out of the equation and see what is going on in our team members' lives. A lot of the time, internal struggles at work are in direct correlation to interpersonal issues. When you can take a step back and understand that the issue is not necessarily the spreadsheet or the project that the team member is working on but a broader situation, you are able to see through that team member's eyes and see how to help them in a different way. This exercise can truly change your relationship with your team. You can also use this activity with your partner, family members, or friends. It is a fantastic way to see and feel the emotions of another human being. Once we do this, our eyesight becomes clearer, and we stop missing the signals and signs that have shown up before.

Seeing your own potential

Chad showed me how I did not want others to feel in my presence. Looking back, I know he was doing his best and trying to figure out his own leadership style while moving up the steps of the corporate ladder at an extremely fast pace. He was one of my greatest teachers, and I know he has learned a lot on his own leadership journey. I have nothing but love and compassion for Chad and have heard that he is now leading teams using a different style and approach.

Once I found Jen and her kind and compassionate leadership style, I quickly learned how to climb up the ladder of empathy and into a new way of being at work. Once I was out of that shame hole and could feel the daylight again, I started to see myself differently. This newfound sight allowed me to feel more empowered, and I was able to give more to myself and to my clients, my colleagues, my friends, and my family.

With this newfound vision, I was able to see and truly help job seekers who were out of work, struggling in their own shame holes, to find their own voice and own their potential. I helped many performers in the Chicago improv community find day jobs where they could make a living during the day and support their creative craft in the evening. I listened to and understood clients' needs and challenges when it came to hiring their teams on a deeper and more meaningful level by putting myself in their shoes.

I was able to help others because I was given the space to do so. I wasn't being trampled on as I was climbing the empathy ladder. I had the freedom and opportunity to go at my own pace and embrace where I was in that moment. I didn't feel trapped in my own hole of shame. I felt as if I had an open field of dreams and opportunities to be creative, and that freedom filled my cup. Since my own cup was filled, I was able to pour into others' and help them find their own independence. This newfound sight was revolutionary to my growth as a professional. It was life changing, and I know it can be the same for you.

You, the visionary

Energy U, you have done a lot in your time here already. You are more than halfway through and have learned how to take care of yourself by setting up routines and habits that lead to the ultimate freedom, self-love. Now that you have these tools in your toolbelt, you have put on a new pair of glasses. Things that once looked fuzzy have now become clearer. Things that you couldn't see far away are now in sharp focus. Like I said, I'm a professor, not an eye doctor, but guess what, my friend: Your vision has improved! You now see how important it is to give to yourself, so you can selflessly give to others. You have passed one of the hardest vision tests of all: seeing yourself as capable of change! This newfound vision has led you to a new title! Energy U, you are now (drum roll, please) . . . a visionary! You can envision a better future for yourself, your team, and the people in your life.

True visionaries help others see their truest potential. When people feel as if they are being championed because they are understood (much like in the empathy activity), all human doing goes out the window, and the focus turns to the highest meaning, the human being. As a newfound visionary, you now see people and yourself in a new and exciting way. Kindness is the root of your being, and you give this to yourself first to give it outwardly to others.

You can also empathize with yourself and others and give grace when needed. Most of all, visionaries showcase love at every level. Let's make one thing clear, visionaries (from here on out, this is your new name): Love and work can go together. And before you put this book down and run away screaming, hear me out: Self-love and outward love are fundamentals of selfless leadership. Make sure to update your LinkedIn profiles and business cards with your new title of visionary. Then connect with me, so I can celebrate who you have become! I SEE YOU!

CHAPTER 9

Interning to an Interview with Barack Obama

"It's already yours."   **–The Universe**

Let's be clear, visionaries: You now have this newfound sight and are eye-mazing. I know these puns are as cornea as they get. As your professor, it's imperative to keep things looking up around here. You wouldn't want me to make a spectacle of myself, would you? I digress, but I must confess that what you will learn in this chapter may be the greatest case study of your newfound gift.

Self-love is an inside job, and it does not happen overnight. It takes a lot of trial and error to really remember who we are and to truly lean into this concept. It starts with taking care of ourselves and our own mental and physical health. As you've witnessed so far, once we lean into these concepts, a new sense of self-love evolves, and you start to become more selfless in your interactions with others. You start to see the world around you differently, with a new sense of sight, and a visionary vision takes shape. This is not an overnight switch. This journey can take weeks, months, and sometimes even years. But the journey back to remembering who you are and truly loving you for you is the fastest path to selfless leadership and a life beyond your wildest dreams. You can find yourself in situations that you could have never imagined possible. Such was the case for Jenna McDonnell.

This case study is imperative on your journey to becoming a selfless leader, and if you can see yourself in the shoes of Jenna McDonnell, you will be able to harness level-ten energy and empathy on a regular basis. Let's dive in, visionaries!

Who is Jenna McDonnell?

Imagine the most kind, caring, and giggly young twenty-year-old woman who loves books, singing, musicals, and learning. She is shy yet confident in her ability to learn. She is quiet, but she knows her own voice (just not how to use it quite yet). She is the meaning of the word *special*. She is special in that her kindness, empathy, and understanding of the world are rare. She has so much potential and talent, and she just needs to learn how to harness it. She sees the best in others and only wants what is of the greatest good. She is an anomaly, a rare find in a world of humans, and you want her special powers around you. The only issue is that she does not yet see how special she is, so your mission is now to help her harness it and see it for herself.

The interview before THE INTERVIEW

Jenna interviewed for an internship at *improve it!* via Skype. This was before Zoom meetings were all the rage. We offered her the position, she accepted immediately, and she showed up on her first day extremely excited but extremely nervous. Her first day was also the last day of a former intern, Rachel, and I was overly emotional at Rachel leaving; she and I had a tight bond. She was leaving to study abroad for the next few months in Rome.

The entire team sat in our lower-level (not to be confused with a basement) office in a coworking space in downtown Chicago. This was huge for the *improve it!* team, because prior to this office, we sat wherever we could in the upstairs lounge of a posh coworking space in the Chicago loop. This lower-level office meant we had made it! We were in the big leagues! We did not have a care in the world that we stuffed four people into a tiny office made for a maximum of two. We complained and joked as we wore winter coats from November to March inside the office because the lower level (not to be confused with a basement) of this coworking space was not insulated. We joked (and were somewhat disgusted) in the spring and summer when we suffered from a gnat problem. Yes, you read that right. We had gnats inside our office, and the coworking space provided us with gnat traps to catch them. We laughed about the fact that we kept our printer in the back maintenance room of the building, because, for some reason, it did not get Internet service in our office.

Even though we did not have the most glamorous of spaces, we felt like having an office meant we were an official business, and we had the happiest, tiniest lower-level (not to be confused with a basement) office in downtown Chicago. We had showtune Fridays, happy hours in the upstairs kitchen, walks to fun lunch spots, and quarterly team building initiatives. It was, to us, perfect.

After getting through her first-day jitters, Jenna contributed to this culture and helped shape it. She loved coming to the office. She loved contributing and seeing the impact of her work. We made it fun, and seeing her have fun made work enjoyable for me and the leadership team.

When Jenna's internship was to end at the end of her senior year, she asked me if she could stay. I told her that we did not have an opportunity to keep her on board, but if she wanted to volunteer to come into the office a couple days a week, we would love to have her. We were a new company, and cash flow was limited (especially now that we were paying for this lower-level office, and we had just hired on a senior leader full time). She happily agreed, telling me this job was "the highlight of her week." I had grown to love Jenna and was so happy to hear she would be coming in. Let it be said that I know the fact that Jenna wanted to volunteer to intern with us is rare and that she was a welcomed anomaly.

Jenna spent her summer applying for jobs and helping in the *improve it!* office two days a week. She commuted from the suburbs of Chicago and gave it her all every time she walked into the gnat-infested, muggy, lower-level office that was definitely not a basement.

On a day when she was not scheduled to be in, she called my phone and told me she had an interview with a company and would like me to be a reference. All at once, my heart sank, and my jaw dropped. I remember exactly where I was at this moment: driving down the road near my apartment in Chicago. As soon as she said, "Will you be my reference?" I swerved the car over to the side of the street and did a parallel parking job that was worse than the one I did on my driving test at sixteen.

We cannot lose Jenna! was the thought racing through my mind as I almost hit a squirrel with my awful parking job. I, of course, said yes to being her reference, and then I unparked my poorly parked car, drove home, and went directly to our budget. If I let go of some of my salary and we adjusted certain line items, we could bring Jenna on part time. There was no one else like Jenna. Her hard work, attention to detail, and kind and compassionate personality made our office the office that it was. She was a wonderful person and made me want to be better. We could not lose her! We must save Jenna!

I called her back the next day to ask her if she would consider part time. Within an hour, she called me back and said yes. I didn't know how we would utilize her talents just yet, but I knew we needed her. She was great with social media, creating documents, research, and editing. She loved comedy, she loved to sing, and she loved to make the world better. All these things were valuable additions to our organization at the time, but there was only one problem. We desperately needed help in the sales department.

I was overwhelmed with day-to-day tasks and could only conduct so many sales meetings per week. Our director of operations at the time was also heavily weighed down with sales and other tasks. Sales would be the answer to helping us move forward, but the problem was Jenna did not know how to do sales and had a severe fear of picking up the phone. A self-proclaimed introvert, Jenna was terrified of conducting sales calls, and the only way to do this was to get over the fear and dive right in.

Now, I'm not talking about a tiny "this seems scary" fear of making sales phone calls. I'm talking about severe phobia. Jenna would pick up the phone and sound as if she was whispering into the receiver. "This is Jenna," she would say more softly than a light breeze. She was so bright and bubbly in person, but once she dialed for a sales call, she did not want to be put on the spot.

We started out by having Jenna do research for prospective companies and setting up meetings for me to take. This was great and worked for a while, until I had officially run out of time in the day for the meetings. I knew Jenna had the power to be a great salesperson due to her empathy and overall ability to truly listen to others. I believed in her; it was Jenna who did not believe in herself.

THE INTERVIEW

Imagine standing onstage, presenting to a room filled with over three hundred people. For some people, this act is a piece of cake. For others, it feels like you are standing naked in front of hundreds of people, vulnerable and afraid. Imagine if one of the three hundred people was a former president, and twenty of the three hundred people were in the media. Would you stand onstage and soak it in or run offstage and hide?

For Jenna, this scenario was as close to a real-life nightmare as she could get. It was 2017, and the *improve it!* team was chosen by the Obama Foundation to train citizens of ages eighteen to twenty-four across Chicago for the first ever Training Day. The mission was to create positive change across the city. My director of talent, Cristy, and I were asked to train a group of twenty-four trainers and then have these trainers help us train the group of two hundred and fifty citizens in a thirty-minute keynote session using improv.

At the time, Jenna was twenty-two, and she was now working part time for *improve it!* We asked our client if Jenna could participate, and the client agreed. Happy and excited, Jenna joined the group of eager citizens on a fall Saturday in Chicago for what would be the experience of a lifetime. The day included a series of breakouts that culminated in brainstorming a project for positive change.

After Cristy and I completed our training of the two hundred and fifty participants, we were asked to go to a room with the rest of the facilitators. As we lined up for a group picture, Barack Obama himself walked into the room. The room burst into cheers, screams, and tears as all the facilitators got to meet and shake his hand. This was a surreal moment, but there was more in store.

The other two hundred and fifty participants (including Jenna) had no idea that they would also be meeting him in just a few moments. They also had no clue that one project chosen from their small groups' collaborations would be presented to the larger audience and would be judged by the former president himself.

The facilitators were asked to reenter the large room where all two hundred and fifty participants were eagerly awaiting their turn to present their projects. The emcee announced the judge of these projects, Barack Obama, and the crowd went wild. As my good friend Barack walked onstage, Cristy and I watched from the back of the room as Jenna jumped up and down with excitement and squealed in delight. We did not know at that time that Jenna's project had been chosen by her group, and she would be presenting her idea.

She was third in line to step up to the microphone. I could feel her nerves, as I knew this was not her cup of tea. I sat in the back of the room with the media, holding my iPhone like a camcorder. (Picture Amy Poehler in *Mean Girls*: "I'm not a regular mom. I'm a cool mom.") As Jenna stepped up to the microphone to pitch her idea to the former president, I took a deep breath and sent her all the love I could. Jenna, who would not even pick up the phone in the *improve it!* office, was about to have a conversation in front of two hundred–plus people with a former president! I sat back and watched her life change before my eyes.

The next ten minutes went by in a blur. I know it's exactly ten minutes, because I have it on video. I had tears streaming down my face as I watched her stand confidently with the microphone, have a back-and-forth conversation with Barack Obama, make him laugh, and have him tell her that her idea was great. As she walked away from the podium and back to her seat, she looked at me with a face that said, "Oh my god!"

As soon as the final project was pitched, the day ended. Jenna ran up to me, and we hugged. Two seconds after our hug, a news outlet approached and asked her for an interview. She was interviewed by several news stations and was the face of the Obama Foundation website for many weeks. She could not believe what happened and was shocked for many days to come.

We joked that if she could have a conversation with a former president in front of a room filled with people, she could do anything. It was an eye-opening experience and a moment of clarity for her. She could see herself as someone who was confident, brave, and willing to get outside of her comfort zone. That moment changed everything about her own vision of herself and the vision she had for her future.

The offer letter to yourself

Because I was working on my own selfless leadership approach, putting energy and effort into showing up as Upward Me, giving to myself first in the mornings, and manifesting what I wanted out of my days, I was able to truly see Jenna. I knew she had the capabilities to be an amazing business development professional, to present to C-level executives, and to make our clients feel seen, heard, and valued. I continued to encourage and support Jenna day in and day out, and it took her seeing and feeling her own brilliance during this experience to really understand this vision.

Soon after the moment with former president Obama, our intern turned part-time employee turned into a full-time employee. She started picking up the phone with confidence, conducting sales meetings like a boss, networking like a professional, and presenting with ease. She quickly changed titles year after year, and she reached revenue goal after revenue goal. She is now the vice president of client experience at *improve it!* and is going on her seventh year with us.

Together, we achieved our best year of revenue yet in 2022. She managed to create partnerships with large names like LinkedIn, Uber Freight, Publicis, Ring, Danone, and Amazon. She's created global partnerships with companies in the United Kingdom and India.

Chances are, if you call into *improve it!* or make an inquiry, you have talked to Jenna. Clients commend her on her attention to detail. She's received compliments like "I thought you were the founder of this company" and "you made me feel like your only client." She is constantly learning and innovating to perfect her craft, and it has been one of the greatest joys of my career to watch her grow. From the shy, timid intern to liaising and conversing with a former president, Jenna McDonnell embodies the mission of *improve it!* to empower yourself to become the best version of you possible.

Now leading our training division and helping lead our internal team, she is on the trajectory for even more growth. She's on her way to becoming president of this company, and it is my mission to empower her to eventually run this division of our business for years to come.

All of this happened because Jenna signed a contract with herself. She accepted the offer letter that life threw her way and signed on the dotted line to a life of self-love and acceptance instead of fear and rejection. I've watched her also sign the contract to her physical and mental health and really put time and energy into personal development each day.

When you accept this offer from yourself, you are signing up for a life beyond your wildest dreams. By trusting in your own power, you are telling the world that you believe you can do anything you set your mind to. Wayne Dyer, an American self-help author and motivational speaker, coined the phrase, "If you believe it, you will receive it." Believing wholeheartedly in your own abilities will offer you up to possibilities you never dreamed of.

So, here's your next step: Write an offer letter to yourself. Come on, newfound visionary. You can do it! Get out a pen and paper or set your fingers on the home row keys and get to typing. What do you want for this next phase of your life? Write out your job description, your salary, where you will be living and working. Write out who you will be working with and how you will feel while working. Then sign on the dotted line, and make it a real contract with yourself.

The result is self-love, acceptance, and abundance in every shape and form. Now, before you roll your eyes and say, "Energy U is getting too woo woo for me," let me remind you of something. Energy is everywhere, and since you are energy, you want to make sure you are emitting the right vibes not only to the people in your life but to the universe. So go ahead: Get out your pen and paper and write that offer letter.

Pro tip: Print the letter out and save it in a safe space in your office or home. Don't look at it for an entire year. Put a reminder in your calendar to come back to the letter one year from when you wrote it. See how much of your offer letter has come true.

In the spirit of vulnerability, I am going to write an offer letter to myself here as an example. Keep in mind that this is an offer letter that I want to happen, and as of the publishing of this book, none of these things have yet to come to fruition. Follow me on my journey to making this happen on any of my social channels (@itserindiehl on Instagram or Erin Diehl on LinkedIn) to see what has transpired by the time you are reading this book.

MY OFFER LETTER

April 12, 2023

Dear Erin Diehl:

Congrats on being a successful author who has changed many lives with your work! You've reached the Amazon Bestsellers list and have rave reviews from many readers that the tangible exercises in the book have shaped their days, therefore helping to shape their lives. People have started to see themselves differently and to accept themselves for who they are, and they have therefore projected this love onto their families, teams, and everyone they encounter. The world feels a bit more kind, compassionate, and empathetic because more people are looking inwardly before giving outwardly! Your team is enjoying many light saver days, you have been thriving with your morning routine (although you don't beat yourself up if you skip a day or two), and you are crushing your days with the iDiehl day methodology.

You have sold over 100,000 copies of your book, and you have a growing and passionate online community of visionaries who deeply care about the world and the people in it. You are still living in your dream location of Charleston, South Carolina, and when you aren't writing or speaking to audiences all over the world, you are enjoying time on the water boating and in the pool with your family and close friends. You work outside some days in the sunshine, enjoy many meals by the grill, and eat the freshest of seafood on the regular (with a side of French fries dipped in a high-quality ranch dressing, of course!).

You work next to your husband most days in your home office and enjoy small breaks in your workday with your son who, when he's home from school, fills the house with joy and love. You feel peaceful and purposeful, and you know your priorities. Your team of amazing human beings

continued

is thriving with workshops and laugh breaks, and you are loving sharing your knowledge with audiences in keynotes. Your days are filled with laughter and copious hugs. You enjoy coffee to start the day and an occasional glass of wine to finish.

There are many benefits to this position, including a casual dress code (real pants are optional), as many vacation days as necessary to spend time with family and friends and to recharge your own batteries, a 401(k), and the opportunity to see, taste, smell, and feel the world through your work travels as a sought-after keynote speaker.

If you have any questions or concerns, please take time to be still and speak with inner management. There will be hard days, but that is where the lessons are learned. The good days will far outweigh the bad, and you can use the lessons you've learned in the hard days to write another book!

We hope you enjoy this position and know you will bring value to it and the world. We see you.

Sincerely,
Your Inner Voice, Inc.

Projection is perception

When you put pen to paper and write out what you believe you can do, chances are you will receive it. Sometimes the timing is exactly when you hoped, but it will eventually come in some way or some form. Put another way, projection is perception. What you project inwardly and outwardly, you will perceive.

Visionaries, you can now perceive yourself in an entirely new light. This newfound sight will shape how you show up to your families, your teams, your clients, your friends. In Jenna's case, it affected how she showed up to a former president! Everyone in your life will benefit from this newfound perception, but most importantly, *you* will reap all the benefits.

This means that the time is now to write your own offer letter and sign on the dotted line to a future of seeing yourself and the world around you differently. If we want to become selfless leaders, we must have instilled in us at our core that we are worthy of greatness.

You can stand on stages; you can converse with former presidents; you can pick up that phone and make that sales call; you can present to anyone at any time; you can get that promotion, buy that car, live in that house, and live those dreams. Project self-love and acceptance inwardly, and you will project love and inclusivity outwardly. Project negativity and rejection inwardly, and you will project limiting beliefs and imposter syndrome outwardly. Which offer letter would you choose to sign?

You: The selfless leader

Selfless leadership starts with radical self-love. You cannot become a selfless leader without first giving to yourself. You must put time, effort, and energy into your own needs first. You know the clichés: Put on your oxygen mask first; fill your tea kettle before pouring into others' cups; give to thee, so ye can truly see . . . OK, so that one is not a cliché—yet! You've witnessed what selfless leadership looks like through the lens of Jen D'Angelo, the opposite of what it is to be led by an unempathetic leader through the story of Chad, and what happens when you allow self-love to transform your own life through the story of Jenna. Jenna's transformation is most demonstrative, as it shows the evolution into the selfless, kind, compassionate leader of *improve it!* she is today.

Selfless leadership is crucial for retaining and attracting top talent and is essential if you want to have a rewarding career filled with service and impact. Just to make sure you fully understand this concept, here are a few examples of how you can demonstrate selfless leadership in your own life.

- Ask a team member how they are doing. When they answer, ask follow-up questions, and truly listen before offering guidance or your own examples.

- Make sure, when having conversations with your team, that you are focused on your own inner tone and dialogue so that you can outwardly project a positive tone.

- Provide examples to your team of your own self-care, such as your morning routine or how you are implementing your iDiehl day, and have them discuss their own implementations. Follow up on these important self-care conversations weekly.

- Slow down when you need to: Be the visionary that the team needs when it comes to taking care of our bodies. When you feel yourself getting sick, slow down and rest.

- Be the example: Take your light saver days, take time off work, set boundaries for work outside of traditional business hours, and be the leader you want to be led by.

- Show the team how to change their mood when they are feeling low with more positive, loving thoughts. Use "New choice!" to call out negative thoughts with the team whenever and wherever you can.

- Find any reason to celebrate. Whether it be a birthday, a work anniversary, a baby shower, a wedding announcement, or a goal achieved, take time out of the workday to do this instead of scheduling it after work. Thirty minutes of intentional support to a team member goes a long way.

- Celebrate the wins: If you use a communication channel such as Slack with your team, create a #winning channel so that your team members can share wins in real time with each other and they can be celebrated. No win is too small to celebrate!

- Give praise when praise is due: Create a #kudos channel in Slack or a shared drive document where team members can give praise to each other in real time for acts of kindness or work well done.

- Get below the surface: Want to really become a selfless leader? Ask your team in one-on-one meetings what drives them. What motivates them? Then truly listen.

- Provide the team with opportunities that fuel their growth and make them feel seen. Does someone on your team have a passion for learning and development? How can you add more of those components into their role? Who can you reach out to about fostering a connection and allowing your team member to learn from them?

- Look out for opportunities for team members outside of their typical scope of work that are aligned with their interests. When you find the right opportunity, do whatever you can to make sure they absorb all they can. Advocating for their growth both personally and professionally will leave a lasting impact on your team member! You never know, they may even write about your leadership in a book one day (wink, wink).

This is part recap of our time together at Energy U and part reminder for you to come back to this when you need examples of how to show up as the leader you want to be. Flag this page, make a copy of it, take a picture of it, put it in your phone, do whatever you need to do to remind yourself that selfless leadership starts and ends with your own reflection of self-love.

PART 3

PART 3

Self-Love +
Selfless Leadership =
A Magnetic Culture

CHAPTER 10

Attractive to Your Core

"Your personal core values define who you are, and a company's
core values ultimately define the company's character and brand. For
individuals, character is destiny. For organizations, culture is destiny."

—Tony Hsieh

Visionaries, take a moment to open your phone, flip it to selfie
mode, and really take a look at that gorgeous vision staring
back at you. Go ahead; give it a go. That vision you see is now seeing
the world and themselves differently. That vision—that sight—is
pure perfection. I want to be friends with that person. Many people
want to know and be around this person. You are thriving, and you,
my friend, are so attractive.

Now, am I being vain in talking about your looks? Of course I
am! Here's looking at you, kid! However, as a professor, it's important
for me to get scientific with this and see all the angles. I'm looking
on the inside here, too, and—what do you know—the inside is even

more gorgeous than the outside. You are radiating light and positive energy and emitting a frequency that could make a paper airplane fly. I hope you are looking at yourself and seeing what I see: pure beauty from the inside out.

You have been diligent now about what you are giving to yourself. You have recognized your tone of voice within, you've given time to just be with light saver days, you've given to yourself in the morning first, redirected your days to become the most iDiehl they could be, and are constantly cleaning up your biggest asset, your mind, with new choices that help you see yourself differently.

All of this glam has been working, my friend. No need for Botox and eyelash extensions; you have changed your appearance from the inside out, and there is not a single filler in the world that could replicate the love that you now have in your own soul.

Through truly seeing yourself, you can see and give energy to others. What you give to others is what magnetizes and attracts people into your orbit, and in your case, as a visionary leader, you magnetize people into your team and organization. Essentially, you are attracting everything you are receiving by giving it outwardly first. Let's dive a bit deeper into this concept.

Your team: A magnetic creation

When you think of a magnetic person, what adjectives come to mind? Go ahead; think of a person you deem attractive. Do not Google them. I need you right here, not going down the IMDb celebrity page rabbit hole. Now, think of a magnetic person you know in real life—someone who is not necessarily famous, but someone who is well known and celebrated in their day-to-day life. What qualities do they possess?

Chances are that this person has a high sense of self-worth and sees themselves in a positive light. By doing so, they can see the light in others, and therefore are able to attract the types of people they want into their orbit. Remember: Self-love and self-worth are inside jobs. And that inside job reflects outwardly. What you give outwardly is what is going to attract and allow those magnets to stick together and create awesome cultures, organizations, and communities.

If you have or know small children, perhaps you've seen the famous toy Magna-Tiles. These are tiles that come in different geometric shapes like squares and triangles with magnets at the edges of the shapes to connect the tiles together. Kids then use the tiles to allow their creativity to flow. They can create buildings, cars, garages, whatever their little hearts desire.

The magnetic tiles attract each other to create beautiful sculptures. It's a collaborative effort on the Magna-Tiles' part, as each individual tile is different and holds a different weight and function in the final masterpiece. When children start building with Magna-Tiles, they lay one piece of foundation at a time. Each tile builds upon the next, and the next, and the next until the child finally finishes building their creation and stands back in awe.

Organizations and teams are just like Magna-Tiles creations. Each person is unique, bringing their own shape and perspective to the collective. Just like Magna-Tiles, you attract the type of people you want and need on your team by emitting the right energy. The current team member who is already a part of the foundation must emit the right energy to the new team member to attract them and have them stick. While team members are emitting their own energy to attract this new Magna-Tile, they are also making sure that the new tile coming into the creation is the right shape and that their magnetic poles are aligned correctly. The new addition to the collaboration should be different and add a unique perspective; however, to add to the overall sculpture, it must understand its function and have a strong belief in what the sculpture brings to the world. It must bring its own set of values but be in line with the core values that the sculpture embodies. That alignment with the vision of the creation is a value add.

Core values are just what they sound like. The values that the sculpture—OK, let's get out of this metaphor now—that the organization believes in. They're what makes the organization function, and they are the core of what the organization offers the world. Let's examine this concept a bit further with a look at *improve it!*'s set of core values.

Lead with *yes, and*

Improve it!'s core values were created by our founding team members. The first is to "lead with *yes, and*." The number-one rule in improv comedy is to *yes, and* one another onstage. This means to postpone judgment of your own ideas as well as others' and, instead of negating any idea, embrace it and add another one on top. This lays the foundation of a scene, line by line—or, in the Magna-Tiles scenario, tile by tile.

As you are aware, I spent many years in improv training, learning from various schools of thought. After not making it into First Municipality, I spent a year and a half of my training at another well-known school of comedy in Chicago. That is where I saw *yes, and* really come to life, and where I met my work partner for life, Cristy Mercier.

Cristy and I met halfway through our classes, and from the moment I first saw her onstage, I was mesmerized by her talent. She was gifted with comedic timing, understood the value of *yes, and*, and never had a bad moment onstage. She was gifted in that she was, herself, hilarious while also making everyone else onstage look good. She created fantastic characters and always made everyone in the class laugh. We became fast friends, and I loved watching her succeed.

After our classes ended, we kept in touch. She did not know I was building *improve it!*, but I knew that she would be the perfect person to help me *yes, and* this idea. One evening, while we were out to dinner, I told her about my concept.

As soon as I told her about the idea for *improve it!*, she quickly said, "Yes! I'm in. This is exactly what I want to do with my life, so let me know how I can help." That was the improviser's way: quick to jump in, *yes, and*, and add value to the scene of life.

As I continued to flesh out the idea, I would ask her for input. She was there for every idea, for every brainstorm, and for the soft launch of our business. Since our inception in 2014, she has now *yes, and*ed our company and brand by not only becoming the senior director of talent but also playing an integral role in our workshops. Cristy not only helped me hire and train all twenty-two of our improv professionals, but she also oversees all the logistics, travel, and training of our programming. She's created our prework videos and countless scripts for Fortune 500 clients for various sketch shows and is my right hand on the facilitation side. She not only *yes, and*ed the idea for our business, but she also *yes, and*ed her life by attracting this dream job to her.

You see, it took my own self-love and belief in myself to come up with the idea for *improve it!*, and because I was loving to myself, I was able to see and appreciate Cristy's talents. Because we were both attracted to the concept, she quickly said, "Yes! How can I help?"

Cristy is the most loyal person, colleague, and friend, and I'm so grateful for the nine-plus years she has given this business. She helped in creating our core value of "leading with *yes, and*," and she embodies this concept daily. Because this is who she is to her core, we attract more facilitators to our organization who lead and facilitate with this mindset. It's a magnetic force that attracts the right types of people into our collaborative creation. Each one builds and *yes, and*s off each other to create the beautiful piece of art that is our company's culture.

Explore more

Improve it!'s second core value is to "explore more." This means to use every day as an opportunity to learn. Essentially, it means to try new things inside and outside of your role. Ask for professional development opportunities, read a book, or take an online course that will further your growth. Outside of your role, this means doing things that will help you continue your growth as a human being, experience opportunities, and enjoy the time away from your laptop. This core value is extremely important, because as lifelong learners, our goal is to always be learning and developing ourselves in any way we can.

One *improve it!* team member, Nicole Entzeroth, has taken this idea and *yes, and*ed it to new heights. Nicole started off as an intern at *improve it!* in 2018. She was a sophomore in college at the time, and from day one, I saw something very special in her. She has an old soul and sees the world through the lens of beauty, love, and compassion. At the time, she handled our social media and helped with other creative endeavors, and she quickly showed her talent as a writer. She brought joy to our tiny, lower-level (not to be confused with a basement) office. No one likes a bragger, but Nicole got to sit in a newer and upgraded lower-level office in Chicago's River North neighborhood, and we had the most gorgeous view of Chicago's ankles. She brought laughter, levity, and positivity to that space, and I, like the rest of the team, was sad when her internship was over.

As time passed, Nicole graduated from her undergraduate program and took a role with Teach for America. After two years of teaching remotely through the pandemic, Nicole was looking for a career change, as well as a remote position. She and her boyfriend were planning to renovate a van and travel the country in it for the next year, and she was looking for a position that would be flexible around her dream.

One fateful day in 2022, while scrolling LinkedIn, I came across a post from Nicole. She mentioned she was looking for a new position that was fully remote. It just so happened that *improve it!* was looking for help with our social media, writing, and other marketing initiatives, and I knew Nicole would add so much value.

We scheduled a Zoom meeting, discussed her travels, and I knew within seconds that we needed her back and that she would make an awesome addition to the team. She quickly came on board, and the rest is history. Nicole is now traveling the country in *Greta Van Fleet*, a vehicle that somehow gets all the best Wi-Fi signals, and stopping in many different cool locations and time zones along the way.

She is thriving because she is living a dream, and we are thriving because, by allowing her to *explore more*, we are allowing her to show up as the best version of herself. Nicole also explores many areas of her role by finding and taking online courses and is constantly tweaking and refining our marketing process.

The entire team was attracted to Nicole's work ethic, and she reentered our Magna-Tiles construct right when we had an opening and needed someone to help us complete the wonderful creation of our culture. Her contribution to our foundation helps us attract clients and partners to our organization, and it's her voice that you hear in many of the marketing initiatives. Although I already knew Nicole, this core value of "explore more" attracted us together at just the right time and completed a missing element of our overall design.

Drive results

Attracting the right people to your organization starts with understanding how you are measuring success. The third core value that we live by is "drive results." It means to create goals that are measured, to break down dreams into actions, and to evaluate each step and adjust as needed. Any goal should be measurable and attainable, and it should be clearly defined.

I've never met anyone who liked a goal as much as me until I met our second intern ever at *improve it!*, Rachel Oliveros. Rachel had her first interview with *improve it!* on the main floor of our first coworking space in downtown Chicago. At this time, we did not have the lower-level (not to be confused with a basement) office and sat with many other entrepreneurs at tables in a communal room. The space was extremely crowded, so we took a two-top table off to the side, which just so happened to be located directly across from the men's restroom. In between toilet flushes, I asked her about her strengths and weaknesses. As we heard the hand dryer go off, she told me about a time she solved a problem at school. We tried to remain professional throughout the interview but eventually just started dying with laughter at the entire situation.

After a moment of flushing and blushing, Rachel said yes to joining us at *improve it!*. Although we are different people, Rachel and I quickly discovered that we shared the same brain. She was a sponge and was extremely quick to learn and absorb information. Give her a goal, and she would make sure she not only hit it but surpassed it. We found joy and delight in setting goals, achieving them, and celebrating our wins. Rachel was still in college, and after spending eight months with *improve it!*, she left for a study abroad program in Rome. The last day of her internship (which was also Jenna's first day, remember), we both spent the day holding back tears. When she walked out the door to go off on her travels, we hugged, cried, and said goodbye. However, we both knew it wasn't goodbye forever, just goodbye for now.

Rachel came back from her study abroad in Rome, graduated from college, and took a position at Paramount. I remained a mentor in her life, guiding her through career decisions, as I knew her dream was to work in the entertainment industry. She quickly received promotion after promotion, as I knew she would.

When we started a podcast at *improve it!* (originally titled *The Failed It! Podcast*), I reached out to her to see if she knew anyone who would want to be our podcast manager. Essentially, I wanted Rachel or her twin, but I knew that she had a full-time job. You can imagine the excitement I felt when she said, "I would love to do this!" For the past three and a half years, Rachel has been with me on the podcasting journey. Every month, we measure our metrics, tweak, refine, and adapt the show as needed to make sure that we bring our *improve it!* peeps the very best in edutainment possible.

With her ambitious drive supporting the show, we have made the show into a top 1 percent global podcast. Our drive and results-oriented approach attracted each of us to working together, and it's honestly a joy to get to work with her on a part-time basis (she still is climbing the ranks at Paramount and continues to drive results there as well). I see you, Rachel! Keep shining!

Play and have fun

Our fourth core value at *improve it!* is to "play and have fun." We encourage embracing your inner child, and as we are teachers of improv comedy, it's a requirement. All twenty-two of our improv professionals embody this fundamental to their core.

Not only do our improv professionals need to have eight-plus years of solid improv experience to facilitate our training, but they must also have a keen understanding of the corporate world and be able to see the correlation between the two. Because this core value is a key component in our hiring process, we have attracted some of the funniest, most hilarious, wittiest, kindest, and most compassionate and caring individuals on planet Earth. We always say that the qualities of a great improviser make up the qualities of a great human, and this is an absolutely accurate assessment. To watch our team interact with one another is pure delight. Your cheeks will hurt from smiling, your eyes will be filled with tears of laughter, and your heart will feel so full.

Anytime I'm lucky enough to be on one of our infamous team road trips, I am fully engrossed in play. I equate driving a car filled with our facilitators to being the ringleader at the circus who is driving the clown car. Each person is *yes, and*ing the person before them, adding to the conversation or the bit, and the outcome is absolute, pure joy. Each team member is completely unique and adds to the conversation in a different way. Each additional *yes, and* packs a punch filled with fun, intelligence, and pure exuberance. It's exciting to witness and a joy to watch.

I wish I had endless space here to share individual stories of these brilliant human beings. They embody the essence of "play and have fun," and they do this day in and day out, onstage and off. We have attracted these brilliant improvisers to our company, and they collectively attract other brilliant minds to our organization simply by being themselves. They are truly the most kind, compassionate, and caring individuals who make fun a part of their every day. What an awesome way to live, and what an attractive quality!

Everyday leadership

Improve it!'s final core value is "everyday leadership." We believe that we are leaders because of our actions, not because of our titles, and we strive to be the leaders that we want to be led by. One of the greatest compliments our team members receive is when a client mistakenly thinks a team member is the founder. This has happened on several occasions with several members of the team. It is my goal for these compliments to continue, because taking ownership of their role not only empowers them to show up as their highest self but also allows them to carry that confidence into the service of others.

As a collective, our team knows that showing up as the highest versions of themselves matters not only on the improv stage but on the stage of life. This means not only doing what is right at any given time but doing what is morally correct in any given situation. I know that our team would act with kindness, love, and compassion in almost any scenario. They would come to someone's rescue if needed, would be honest, and would do what is of the highest good for all involved. The core value of "everyday leadership" is the root of every team member at *improve it!*, and it makes our team the picturesque, abstract, Magna-Tiles tower that it is.

Each individual piece is unique and different, and we celebrate those differences. But each piece attracts the others, using the underlying magnets of our core values. When we magnify our strengths and values, an energetic force bigger than us takes over. You can feel this energy radiate as we collectively magnetize together to enter the rooms of the teams that we serve. That energy, that magnetic pull, is what changes the people within these rooms. Everyday leadership means exactly what it says: showing up, every single day, as the leader we wish to be led by.

Stick to your core

The five core values mentioned above are the pillars that we use to hire, maintain, and attract new talent. Let it be known that I did not create these core values alone. They were collectively created by our internal team and then used as a measuring stick for hiring and a guideline for performance, and they are used as our calling card when it comes to serving our clients.

Core values are the foundation of a strong team, a strong organization. If you do not have core values in place for your organization, the next set of activities are for you. Or, perhaps you have core values set in place for your organization, but they are out of touch with the current team. If so, it's time for a refresh! Finally, if you have core values as an organization but you would like to create a set of core values exclusively for your team, the following activities will help. Final-finally (I promise, it's the last one), if you want to create a set of core values for yourself to live by, this next set of activities are for you. Basically, do the following activities, visionaries. You will see what I mean once you've completed them!

Solo activity: Working on your core

Step 1: Gather your materials for this activity. You will need a timer, a sheet of paper, and a pen.

Step 2: Set the timer for five minutes, and without judgment, write down any word that comes to mind to describe your own personal core values. Write as many words as possible, without self-censoring, and don't stop until the timer goes off. Examples: adventure, family, fun, mindfulness, play, etc.

Step 3: After five minutes, look at the list of core values you've created. Set your timer again for five minutes, and without judgment, circle your top five core values. Take the full five minutes to think these through.

Step 4: Look at your top five core values and write them down at the top of your paper.

Step 5: Choose three people in your life who you know extremely well, and ask them to give you a list of five words to describe you. An easy way to do this is to send a quick text that says "Hi, Susan! I'm working on developing my core values for a project I am working on at Energy U. Could you send me a text back with five words that you would use to describe me? I'll explain what Energy U is later." (You can take or leave the Energy U part, but you get the idea!)

Step 6: Once you get your list of five words that describe you from three friends, compare their words with your list. Do any of them have crossover or the same meaning? Using your list, as well as comparing the lists from your closest peeps, compile your top five core values into one final list.

Step 7: Here's where you can get your creative juices flowing. Create catch phrases for the five words to use as your list of core values. For example, let's say one of your collective five words was *fun*. Your catch phrase could be "I see every day as an opportunity to have fun" or "I measure my success by the amount of fun that I am having." The catch phrase uses the word to create a sentence—a tweetable, if you will. Keep your core values short, sweet, and under 280 characters. In other words, the shorter the better!

Group activity: Group core workout

Step 1: Have everyone complete the solo activity above before meeting collectively as a group.

Step 2: Conduct a group meeting, and have everyone bring their results from the solo activity.

Step 3: Using the core words instead of core phrases (your answers from step 7 above), appoint one team member as the scribe to take notes. You will need either a shared screen or a large marker board for this next section of the activity.

continued

Step 4: Go around the group, and one at a time, have each individual share a core value. The scribe writes down the core value (one word only) on the shared screen or marker board. As the group continues to share words, have the scribe start to compile the words into buckets.

For example, let's say that individuals in the group say words like *fun*, *adventure*, *spontaneity*, and *play*. These words are grouped together in their own bucket because they are all synonyms. Another example would be words like *professional*, *practical*, and *punctual*. These words would be grouped together, because they collectively mean the same thing.

Step 5: Keep this going until everyone has shared all five of their words and buckets of similar words have started to fill. As a group, look at the buckets. What is the theme of each of them? Write that core word at the top. It is all right to use one of the words listed in the bucket! Note that the goal would be to have five or six buckets that are then distilled into five to six core words. These words now become the starting place to brainstorm your collective catch phrases.

Step 6: Starting with the first bucket, have the group brainstorm catch phrases for each core word. So let's say the first bucket's core word was *play*. A catchphrase could be "Play, learn, and have fun," just like you see in the *improve it!* core values. Do this for all your core words, and make sure that everyone has a chance to share their ideas.

Step 7: Now that you have your collective catch phrases, it's time to create tag lines underneath. For the catch phrase of "Play, learn, and have fun," our tagline is "We encourage embracing your inner child." This is much less important than the catchphrase itself, but it is important in helping support the main idea. Keep the taglines short and sweet.

Step 8: Now that you have all the collective core values listed as catch phrases and taglines created under each one, create a document that lists the core values. A fun place to do this is on a software system like Canva, where you can use visuals to get creative and showcase your collective brainstorm. Place them on your internal drives or in your physical office if you have one, and be extremely proud of what you have created.

Go to itserindiehl.com/resources to get your downloadable *I See You! Guidebook*.

Your magnetic muscle

You didn't know there would be a workout involved at Energy U, now did you? I know you've learned a lot and are mentally exhausted, but you're doing it, visionary! You have gotten in the reps and are now ready to strengthen that magnetization muscle. You've put the time and effort into yourself by recognizing your own set of core values. Great job, visionary. You've used this self-realization to help you create a set of guiding core values for your team, where they have contributed to the creation and have felt seen, heard, and valued in the process. You are a selfless leader!

Now you are magnetizing the right people to your organization using these tools and not only helping them reap the benefits of the positive energy you've created but also helping them stay awhile. Grow, learn, fail, tweak, adopt, and refine as needed, but your set of magnetic vibes has staying power. Give yourself some love for working your brain and creating a mind-meld of marvelous magnetic souls. You are doing the work, visionaries, and your vision is coming to life. I see you!

CHAPTER 11

Magnetizing Missionaries

"Outstanding people have one thing in common:
an absolute sense of mission."

–Zig Ziglar

Visionaries, now that you are aware of your magnetic capabilities, let's stick it all together. Because you are now a selfless leader who applies radical self-love to your own life, you are now visualizing and magnetizing your future and your future team. You have a high sense of self-awareness using all the self-love tools we've learned along the way. This helps you show up day in and day out as the selfless leader you want to be led by. Because you have guided your team to understand their own individual set of core values, you, the visionary, now have missionaries to help carry out your vision.

Here's the deal, visionaries. Your missionaries are not delivering the gospel. They are delivering the elements of humanity that all teams and organizations should spread. These are the elements of kindness, compassion, and love. These are the underlying fundamentals of the humankind gospel that you spread from human to human, team member to team member. Layer on top of this foundation the mission of your team or your organization, the vision and plan that you, collectively, have created. These missionaries see the vision, and their job is to fulfill it and spread the word far and wide.

The missionaries use the gravitational pull from your core values to pull together every task and every interaction internally and externally. The missionary's job is to take what you, the visionary, have described, *yes, and* it with aligned ideas, and then act toward achieving the goal. The missionary is on a mission because you have helped them see their own potential and empowered them every day to do so. When you use the core values as the source for hiring and maintaining top talent, the missionary will always be in line with the mission.

When you hire using your core values as the framework, you know that the person you are bringing into your organization is in line with your mission. You know that, even though they may not possess all the skills that are needed to perform the job, they are trainable, are moldable, and can learn. Your core values, otherwise known as *soft skills*, are one of the hardest things to teach, and this is why *improve it!* exists. Most soft skills, or as I like to call them, *power skills*—are the residual effect of patterns set in our formative years of life. When you hire someone who does not have the same value system as your organization, you will spend more time worrying and complaining about this aspect of their contribution instead of teaching them skills with the already engrained set of core values.

For example, let's say you want to hire someone in business development for your organization. The values of your organization are set in place, so for the purpose of this example, we will use *improve it!*'s set of core values. Just a quick reminder: These are "lead with *yes, and*"; "explore more"; "drive results"; "play, learn, and have fun"; and "everyday leadership." You post a position for the business development role and narrow it down to two candidates. One candidate has a great professional network and has been in a sales role for many years. They know how to do the job and can do it with ease.

However, as you go through the interview process, you realize that this person does not lead with *yes, and.* They seem very siloed instead of collaborative, which is one of your underlying values. As the interview process continues, you realize that this person does not enjoy working with teams, and even though you know that they can perform and drive results, you are not seeing examples of collaboration and everyday leadership. Would you hire this person just because you know they could increase revenue with their network of professionals and impact the bottom line?

Really think about your answer here.

As their leader, would you spend more time course correcting this person on how to work with the team that already exists? The answer is most likely yes. If you allow this person to work in a silo and to not effectively communicate with your preexisting highly functional and collaborative team, you are creating a disconnect between your words, values, and actions.

The preexisting team will notice this disconnect, and it will eventually lower morale. Once morale is lowered (and work becomes a never-ending cycle of problem-solving due to the team's faltering dynamics), does it really matter that your new hire is impacting the bottom line when your core values and mission have completely dissolved?

Every person you allow into your organization should want to fulfill the role of the missionary and should strongly believe or support the core values set in place. This is measured before the new hire is onboarded, in the interview process, and is the driving metric when it comes to performance. This takes intentional effort, time, and continuous review. Let's look at this a bit further.

Understanding the mission

Now that you have the core values set in place for your team and/ or organization, it's time to put them to work. The next time you are hiring a new team member, incorporate the core values into the hiring process. Not only do those core values automatically qualify as behavioral interview questions, but they also show you right away whether the interviewee connects and accepts the mission to come on board. This may sound daunting, but there are simple and easy ways to do this.

At *improve it!*, we create pre-interview sheets for each current team member to use as a guide when we are hiring a new team member. We create interview questions based on the core values, and we make sure to spread the questions out among our team members, so that the interviewee does not hear the same question twice. This is a great opportunity to have different conversations with the candidate and for the candidate to obtain a deeper understanding of *improve it!*'s mission. Below are a few examples of how we incorporate the core values questions into the interview process:

- "Lead with *yes, and*" is one of our top core values. How do you incorporate *yes, and* into your day to day?

- "Play, learn, and have fun" is one of our core values. What do you do for fun and to release your inner child?

- "Explore more" is one of our core values. How do you incorporate learning new things into your life?

- "Drive results" is one of our core values. What are some of your biggest goals you've ever accomplished, and how did you achieve them?

- We also practice "everyday leadership." How would you define your leadership style, and how do you prefer to be led?

- Which one of our core values do you hope to exhibit in this job?

Prior to the interview, the candidate receives a pdf of the core values, and we let them know that this will be a central element of the interview process. The questions are then split among team members during the interview process, and then we use a metric system to tally the results. Prior to asking questions surrounding the core values, we will ask questions regarding the role the candidate is being hired for, their knowledge of soft skills (huge when you run a soft-skill training company), and then the core values questions. We then measure on a 1–5 scale—1 being low and 5 being high—their energy and enthusiasm, their desire to serve others, their desire to learn, and their basic understanding of our core values. After the interview and after the candidate has met with several team members, we tally up the interview scores from each team member and give the candidate an overall score. Our core values are heavily weighted.

If we are confused or concerned about whether to move forward with a candidate, we use one final deciding factor in the interview process, which doesn't come down to skill set at all. We call it "the airplane test." It is a very simple concept. If we sat next to this person on an airplane for eight hours, would they be kind, compassionate, and empathetic? We are in the business of people, so if we do not feel warmth, kindness, or compassion from this individual, they will not showcase this to the people we serve. Not to mention, a lot of our work involves flying in airplanes to work with teams, so it is important to know that the person we are hiring would demonstrate love and empathy while flying 30,000 feet in the air.

When it boils down to it, making sure your new hires understand the mission, the why, and the values behind it are more important than any other skill. Teaching someone a software system is much easier than teaching them kindness. Teaching someone how to sell is much easier than teaching them how to truly be empathetic. Missionaries are there to help fulfill the mission of the organization, and without a complete understanding of the mission, they will never complete it.

Measuring against the mission

Now that you have hired your team using this set of guiding values and the team is on board with the mission, it's time to measure their success. One way to do this is through performance reviews. Every company and organization has their own standard when it comes to measuring performance.

Many organizations conduct 360 degree reviews with managers and peers, which means compiling feedback from direct reports, senior leaders, and cross-functional colleagues. Some organizations do direct-report performance reviews only, meaning that the leader gives feedback to their employee. Whatever your organization uses, here is a simple and efficient way to measure performance using your set of core values. Keep in mind that if you hire your missionary using this set of principles, this performance review will be a recap of past conversations and should be a review of how well the candidate is measuring up to the expectations you set upon hiring them. Let's walk through conducting this performance review step by step.

STEP 1

Decide a cadence for your team's performance reviews. At *improve it!*, we now do biannual reviews in June and December. Decide what makes sense for you and your team, and schedule time on the calendar for the reviews.

STEP 2

One week prior to the review, send your team the performance review sheet. I've included it in the downloadable guide found at www.itserindiehl.com. It's simple and effective and leads to great conversations.

STEP 3

Complete the performance review for your direct reports, as well as for yourself. This is crucial; you, the leader, also need feedback on how you are measuring against the mission. Here's how to complete it.

For each core value, measure the performance of the team member for the period from your last review to now. Rate the team member on a scale of 1–5 in terms of how they have successfully measured up to that core value over the allotted period. A score of 1 means that there is very little understanding and implementation of the core value, a score of 3 is average, and a score of 5 is above average. You can also give half scores, but just keep in mind that the number 5 means mastery of the core value.

Next to the score column, you will see a space for comments. Make sure to write comments to remind yourself why you gave this score to the team member, because the reason for the score is the most important part. For example, you may give someone a 5 for "driving results." In the comments section, list the things that they have done that demonstrate their results, such as hitting all their sales goals, increasing the newsletter's numbers, or bringing in the number of candidates needed if in a recruiting role. Rate the team member, then do the exact same thing for your performance.

STEP 4

On the day of the review, make sure to be in a quiet, uninterrupted space. If you are conducting the review virtually, make sure to use headphones and avoid being interrupted. Close all tabs on your computer, silence your phone, and give your full attention to the person you are speaking with.

STEP 5

Start by asking the team member if they have any questions. Then, have them go through their core values sheet with you, and allow them to rate themselves. After each individual core value, allow them to say how they think they measured against it. Then give your score, as well as the commentary to that core value. Do this for each individual core value until they are all complete. Allow room for discussion.

STEP 6

Now, do all of this in reverse, so that you are giving yourself feedback. Go through each individual core value, provide your response, and then allow the team member to provide you with theirs. This is crucial, to allow your team members an opportunity to provide you with feedback. Sit, listen, and take it all in. Make sure to have a notebook handy to take notes.

STEP 7

Create an action plan for both you and the team member. Now that both of you have had an opportunity to rate each other's performance, create a three-step action plan for the next six months (or however long you have decided for your next review) to improve performance.

Performance review review

Chances are, if you have hired the correct team member, they will always fall between average (a score of 3) and above average (a score of 5). This is great; you'll know that the team is connected to the values and the mission and is ready to serve others. The other wonderful thing about this practice is that it not only carves out time and a safe space for you to provide feedback, but it also provides an opportunity for the team members to provide *you* with feedback. This is huge, because most of the time, team members feel reluctant to manage up.

By giving the opportunity for feedback to the team, you are showcasing not only that you are willing and able to listen to constructive feedback but also that you are open to improvement, to creating positive change. You are showing your team that you are mission critical and letting them know that you are always open to growth and learning opportunities. It is a fantastic practice and keeps everyone accountable to upholding and uplifting the core values so that you can carry out the mission of your team and organization with grace and ease.

Mission never complete

Now that you have magnetized a diverse group of people with different skill sets who share an underlying set of strong core values into your organization, you have attracted the right people to help spread the greatness that is your work. This is mission critical if you want to spend less time teaching the individual underlying skills such as empathy, kindness, and compassion.

In the long run, you have essentially saved yourself time, effort, and energy. Since you have clearly defined the values upfront, you will save time on problem-solving and spend more time focusing on the actual work. You've established these fundamentals from day one, and they are laid out as the foundation and the expectation of performance.

Speaking of performance, you have laid out clear expectations for the behaviors that you know are critical to the mission of your organization, and you've set time on the calendar to measure your performances against them. Because you have attracted different types of people with the same set of core values, you have an eclectic arrangement of human beings who care about putting energy into themselves so they can serve the world as selfless leaders. While you, the visionary, are creating and innovating, the missionaries are implementing the tasks needed to complete the mission.

Essentially, visionary, your mission is never over. There is always more to put into the world, more to give, and more to create. However, when there is a keen understanding and constant measurement of your core values, your heart will feel complete knowing that you have the right people in place to move the mission forward. Together, you and this forcefield of energy workers will continue to put the right energy into yourself so that you can give the right energy out into the world. That energy that you collectively give will mirror back to you the qualities you have put out. You are a MAGNET, and there is no better feeling than watching the reciprocal effect of your vision pull together.

CHAPTER 12

You Are a MAGNET

"There is a magnet in your heart that will attract true friends. That magnet is unselfishness, thinking of others first; when you learn to live for others, they will live for you."

–Paramahansa Yogananda

Visionaries, you have been putting in the work and effort, and it shows! You have realized that by putting energy into yourself, you are showing up as the selfless leader you are meant to be. By doing this, you are magnetizing and attracting the right people into your organization, as well as keeping them energized and functioning at their highest levels. You're a visionary, and you've compiled your team of missionaries to help spread your mission far and wide. You are a MAGNET.

Now, you've been a part of Energy U long enough to know that I love any tool that helps you learn faster and helps the concept stick. So, *What is a MAGNET?* you ask. Such a great question. This means

you *magnetize and attract a great network where everyone thrives.*
Pretty memorable acronym, huh? Energy U is a clever place, and
since you are a student for life, it's important to give you a tool that
you can easily remember.

When you understand your own self-care and how to really commit to loving yourself, you can then give this energy outwardly. It's
selfless leadership at its finest. Once you give out the frequency of
kindness, compassion, and empathy to your team, this electric force
will have no choice other than to spill over to the humans you are
serving. Once your team feels safe and supported, they will be able
to serve others using this energy. Then, you will be able to magnetize and attract the right customers, clients, partners, and vendors
into your organization. The electric force emitted to the world is
so strong. You see, this electric force starts with you, Energy U. You
must give this love, this energetic pull to your own mind first. By
magnetizing self-love to yourself, you internalize it and then can
attract others using this selfless leadership tactic.

Once you attract others, you create a great, gigantic network of
selfless leaders who are inspired to carry out the mission set out by
you, the visionary. This magnetic force of people driving toward the
same goal attracts others. People want to be led and coached by your
selfless leadership. They want to buy from you, learn from you, and
stand next to you on this mission to serve the world.

Because the missionary believes in the work to their core, the
audience that is being served believes in it too. Vendors and partners are attracted to your mission and want to help it succeed. This
MAGNET approach is only complete if you, the selfless leader and
visionary, put time, effort, and energy into yourself. It's circular: You
start with self-love and, by doing this, you can give more to your
team. The team feels this energy, this selfless leadership, and feels
seen, heard, and valued. Because they are strong believers in the core

values you are striving for and the mission you are working together to achieve, they can share this mission with the world. These missionaries then attract the clients, buyers, vendors, and partners that your business needs to thrive.

Keep in mind that it all starts with you. You are the driving force behind the MAGNET approach. There is no other driving force than you, the visionary, reading and listening to these words. If you believe internally, it will show externally, and everything in your life will feel seamless and easy.

Upset U did not understand this concept of being a MAGNET. Upset U had no idea how to put time, effort, and energy into themselves. Upset U had no idea how to magnetize or attract anything except more frustration and pain. It took a reflection on how you were spending your time, starting your mornings, and going about your days to redirect yourself into Upward U.

Now the realigned, more focused Upward U puts intentional effort into your mornings, cares about and works toward manifesting your iDiehl day, and has a keen awareness about your body. Upward U makes sure that your light does not burn out by implementing light saver days. Upward U can see themselves differently and, through that lens, is able to view your team differently.

Through this lens, a selfless leader is born. You are then able to create and implement core values that magnetize and attract the greatest, most aligned missionaries. You, the visionary, are fulfilling your mission, living it to its fullest, and being the best example of a MAGNET to others. See how this comes full circle, visionaries? It took us a few chapters to get here, but now you understand your assignment. You are so close to graduating from Energy U and carrying out these principles daily. But before we go, we must make sure you understand a few more very important concepts. Let's get to it!

You can ask for help

By standing true in your power and using this MAGNET energy as a microphone to the world, you can not only magnetize clients, partners, and team members into your organization, but you can magnetize the right coaches and mentors to help you along the way. Because you understand your own self-worth, are in alignment with your own self-care, and can project that outwardly, you attract the mentors and coaches who can help you get to the next level. You are no longer playing small, visionary. Your frequency is now so powerful that it cannot go the road alone.

Every visionary needs a coach to help them stay focused and in alignment with their core values and mission. Investing in yourself and attracting the right mentor into your life will change the course of your leadership. Because of the weight you now carry as a visionary, you will need another visionary in your life to help you see the blind spots—the areas in your leadership and in your business that need improving. Do not be wary of this, visionaries. It is vital for your success!

I could not be the professor that I am today without the leaders and mentors that I've invested in. For example, while creating this curriculum for you, I have a writing coach and a digital course I am taking, as well as a speaking coach and a life coach who help me see the world differently.

I understand that having these mentors is a privilege, but *improve it!* would not be anywhere near where we are as an organization, and I would be unable even to create the words on this page, without their guidance. Most importantly, I know that these are the *right* mentors for me at exactly the right time.

Each mentor is in alignment with my core values. Because I have completed the inner work and have truly started to love myself, I am able to project that same love to them. That energy attracted these mentors into my life. Without the digital course and mentorship of Gabby Bernstein, I would have no idea how to put words to paper or fingers to home row keys to write this Energy U curriculum. Without my speaking coach, Jane Atkinson, I would be clueless when it comes to all of the elements that make up a great keynote speech. Without my intuitive life coach, Michael Frontier, I would have never been able to uncover some of the unprocessed emotions that kept me creatively blocked. As a visionary, I know that I need people who are smarter than me and brilliant at their craft to help me through this journey of writing the Energy U curriculum for you.

As a visionary, asking for help is the single most important way to thrive. Asking for help does not make you weak; it does not make you small. It makes you much stronger and expands you in a way you could not do alone. Before committing to a coaching or mentor relationship, make sure that the people you are bringing into your orbit are in line with your core values. Once you establish that alignment, your assignment will flow naturally and with ease.

High VIBES

Visionaries, just when you didn't think it was possible to drop another acronym on you, I'm coming in hot with one more. This may be one of the most important ones yet, so get ready for your mind to be blown. This frequency, this aura, this light that you are expanding out to the universe around you creates high VIBES. This means that you not only talk the talk, but you walk the walk—the walk of a visionary and selfless leader. It means you are a _very important believer in energetic significance_. You see, feel, and sense with a heightened awareness of your own energy and the energy around you.

With this newfound shift in perception, you might find that you have outgrown certain people in your life and that their own frequency is not a match for your VIBES. You might be led by a Chad and realize that life is just too short for this type of energy and do everything you can to find a Jen. This newfound sight might make you realize that the people you lead are no longer a match for the mission and your core values, and you might decide to part ways. On the other hand, you may realize that a person on your team adds so much value and is so aligned with your core values that you will go to great lengths to retain them.

This new way of seeing and interacting with the world will take time to adjust to. It's like putting on a new set of glasses with a stronger, more focused prescription. It's a little weird at first—you might get a headache—but the sharper focus helps you see clearer in the long run. You might feel inclined to put on the old pair of glasses and go back to your way of viewing the world, but trust me when I say that things will not look and feel the same. This new vision and way of feeling VIBES is a clearer, more focused way of living and will help you see what you want and don't want out of work—and, ultimately, your life.

Protecting your VIBES

Because your magnetic power is so strong, you will start to find that a lot of people want to be in your presence. There may be many Upset Thems who want to feel your Upward U VIBES and hope that by just being in your presence, you can change the way that they feel and see the world. Be cognizant of the people you interact with who increase your VIBES and leave you feeling more energized and fueled. Notice the people who lower your VIBES and make you feel exhausted and depleted. You will know exactly when this happens because you will feel the shift in yourself. You will feel your own VIBES start to diminish, and you will go back to Upset U patterns.

When you feel this energetic shift, here's an immediate thing to do to protect your VIBES. Immediately imagine yourself wrapped in a cape. Think of this cape as a cape that a superhero wears to show off and protect their powers. Imagine the back of the cape has the words *ENERGY U* on it in big, bold, capital letters.

Let's imagine that you are about to have a meeting with someone who you know has Upset U tendencies and will lower your VIBES. Put on your Energy U cape and wrap yourself in it tightly. Imagine yourself being enclosed inside it. Give the cape a color (mine is teal), and wrap yourself snugly in this beautifully colored piece of cloth. Feel the warmth of the cape, and tell yourself, "I am safe. I am loved." Then walk into the meeting with the Upset U knowing that your own VIBES are protected. Be your loving, kind, and compassionate self, but don't let the UPSET U steal your energy.

In many cases, this Upset U will be triggered by your own vibration and will try to stop at nothing to lower it. Your Energy U cape will not allow the Upset U to take down the positive self-love that you have worked so hard for. The invisible cape is your shield, and that shield will protect your energy in times of need. By raising this shield, you can stand tall in your power and give out the selfless leadership VIBES that you have worked so hard to create. Your Energy U cape is always there for you, in whatever moment, when you need it. So, the next time you are engaging with an Upset U and you start to feel your energy shift and drain, throw on your cape, stand tall in your power, and know you are protecting your own energy and strength.

Activity: Stand in your high VIBES

Now that you have a tool to use anytime your energetic bound-aries are crossed, I've got one more to put in your Energy U toolkit. Below is a tool to use when you want to ramp up your Upward U energy. The following activity can be done alone or with a group, but it is best completed in a safe and quiet space. Let's rev up your visionary VIBES, shall we?

Step 1: Grab a timer and stand with your legs straight and your arms at neutral.

Step 2: Set your timer for three minutes.

Step 3: While standing, find a position with your body that makes you feel powerful. It could be standing with your hands on your hips, standing with your legs open and arms high above your head in a letter V, or standing with your arms wide open in a T. Find a pose that is comfortable to you but that, above all, makes you feel like you can do anything.

Step 4: Hold this pose for the full three minutes.

Step 5: Release the pose, and examine your VIBES by answer-ing the debrief questions below.

Activity debrief

Question 1: How did you feel after standing in this pose for three minutes?

Question 2: What did this pose do to increase your VIBES?

Question 3: How can you use this newfound increase in energy to go about your day?

Question 4: How can you incorporate this activity in the latter part of your day, when you feel your VIBES start to shift?

Go to itserindiehl.com/resources to get your
downloadable I See You! Guidebook.

You oversee your VIBES

If you want to magnetize the right clients, partners, mentors, and coaches into your life, you must believe in your own power and your own magnetization abilities first. Once you believe and trust in your own VIBES, you are free. This freedom and newfound confidence will change your life. You will no longer worry about how you are going to show up, who will be there, how you will appear. You will no longer feel drained or depleted, and you will no longer carry the frenetic energy of Upset U. You will feel a sense of inner peace and ease and will carry this energy into your leadership capabilities. This sense of calm will allow you to innovate and create at the highest visionary level, encourage the missionaries to bring your vision to life, and help you attract the right clients, partners, and mentors to support you.

When we own our VIBES, we magnetize others who have the same frequency. These people support our mission and help us carry out the goals and assignments that we are here to do. When we stand in our power instead of diminishing it, we understand that we are in complete alignment with our assignment. Your friendly neighborhood webbed man once said, "With great power comes great responsibility." Now that you know and accept this power, you can embrace it to help change the world.

We have a choice in how we leave the world. Why not leave it a kinder, more loving, and more compassionate place? Why not spend your time here empowering yourself and others through selfless love, leadership, and light? Why not choose to see the light in ourselves so we can give that light to others? When we choose this path, we have true vision. What a sight, and what a gift to *truly see*.

CHAPTER 13

Energy U Commencement Speech

"Everything is energy and that's all there is to it. Match the frequency of the reality you want, and you cannot help but get that reality. It can be no other way. This is not philosophy. This is physics."

–Darryl Anka

As your wacky, cool-mom professor, I am sad to say that all great things must come to an end. Visionaries, you have learned so much during our time together. You took the curriculum that you didn't know you were already studying, added in new layers and lessons, and have accelerated yourself to today. This is the most special of days: graduation day. It's a day that will live on forever as you take the tools that you have been given and implement them every moment of every day into the future. When plotting out how I was going to send you back into the world, I knew that there was only one way to give you the speech of all speeches. Because nothing is conventional here, I knew it had to be in the form of a poem.

So, visionaries, I want to invite you to sit back, relax, and let the rhyming begin as you hear the speech of all speeches to send you on your way. This talk is here to send you out into the world as the visionary, self-loving, selfless leader superstar you are.

Ahem, ahem (that was me clearing my throat). Here we go, visionaries.

Energy U commencement speech: A poem

You started off as a lifelong student at Energy U
You didn't know you were already formally enrolled; this much is true

As time went on, it was made clear
That you needed this master class in love; it was time to stop living in fear

You came in unsure but knew you would learn a ton
With a wacky professor leading the way, I'm sure you knew that we would incorporate fun

You witnessed the juxtaposition of Upset and Upward U
And learned how to listen to yourself and help your mind and body renew

You can now say yes to you with ease and grace
No more burning the candle; gone is that negative space

You know how to plan light saver days to savor your light
And now you know how to fill your cup first. What a delight!

By saying yes to yourself and your iDiehl day
You run your life; chaos and stress no longer have a say

When you find yourself thinking negative thoughts and have
a limiting belief
You can say, "New choice!" and choose again. What a relief!

You can now empower yourself and your team to think
about their favorite things instead of gripe
This is all because you are now a visionary; you know your
type

A selfless leader who leads with the energetic level of ten
When your selfless leadership ways start to fade, reread the
story of Jen

You now know how to use empathy to cheer others up when
they are sad
Make sure to remember the lessons we learned from our
boy Chad

You've written your offer letter to yourself as the smart, selfless leader you are
I don't have to tell you this, visionary, but you are a star!

Because you've put love inwardly, outwardly it shows
And because of this selfless leadership, a magnetic culture
begins to flow

Your Magna-Tiles culture creation is beautiful, with each
piece different in shape, color, and size
Then you got to witness your core values start to take shape
right before your very eyes

Once your core values and your teams are aligned
You start to attract the right people and develop group mind

As the visionary, you are creating and innovating day after
day
Your missionaries are the mouthpiece, showing the world
your combined way

You hire and measure performance based on who your team is at their core
Because of this magnetic attraction, so much goodness is in store

You are a MAGNET, and your network is strong and vibrant
You are attracting others who also understand their value, as well as their own assignment

You have high VIBES and now know how to protect your energy with a swift fling of your cape
When you feel the Upset Us try to steal your energy, it's time to escape

Standing tall in your power, you have the self- and outer love to give to those you lead
With a deep understanding of these principles, you will succeed

So, visionaries, former students of Energy U
It is now time for me to bid you adieu

Your time here has come to close, but know this is not goodbye
You will see me in only a wink of an eye

Your sight is now so strong that it's time for you to help others see
Congrats on becoming the visionary you were destined to be

You are confidant, powerful, and a force; it's true
These are traits you once weren't sure of, but we always knew

Now find a mirror and smile at the visionary in your reflection
Look closely, my friend, and you will not find one imperfection

Take a deep breath in, smile, and look at this gorgeous view
Now tell yourself with pride, "I love you, and I see you."

Once this is complete, your graduation is through
Congratulations! You are officially an alumni of Energy U

(Insert fireworks.)
(Insert confetti guns.)
(Insert the band playing.)

Now the real work begins. Go change the world, visionary. And know that if you ever lose your way, you have an army of like-minded, kind, compassionate, and empathetic missionaries and visionaries behind you. We will be right here—loving, supporting, and cheering you on, today and always.

I see you, visionary.

I see you.

Acknowledgments

This book would not be possible without the many incredible people in my life who truly see me.

First, I want to thank my mom and dad for procreating and allowing me to own my weird. You never told me I could not be who I want to be, and that type of *yes, and* in my formative years is what lead me to improv. Thank you for allowing our living room to be my stage and for watching me pretend to be Mark Summers, the host of Nickelodeon's hit eighties show *Double Dare*, for hours on end. You allowed me to pretend to be every version of myself I could imagine, and for that, I am truly grateful.

To my brother, Jon, who allowed me to dress him in all my old dance costumes and took on every character I ever asked. I'm sorry that my own character took a turn through puberty, and I'm so glad we are good friends in our adult years and that you have found such a wonderful partner and a great sister-in-law for me in Shelly.

To the great leaders, coaches, and teachers who helped me on my own leadership path, especially Jen D'Angelo, who showed me what selfless leadership looks and feels like. Jen, you will always be a huge chapter in my book, literally and figuratively. The world needs more you!

To the team at *improve it!* There are no words for how grateful I am, but I guess acknowledgement sections make you find them.

Jenna, you are *improve it!* You are the mission, the case study, the muse. You inspire me every day to become a better person, and I have learned more than you'll ever know by watching you grow into the beautiful professional woman you are.

Cristy, thank you for believing in me and this vision, even when I didn't fully believe in myself. Thank you for witnessing my Tory Burch moments and all the wonderful ones in between. I am so grateful for all you do for our team and this business. I cannot wait to see what the future holds!

Rachel, thank you for taking an internship even while toilets flushed outside of our interview space and for being the best podcast manager on planet Earth. Please continue to keep me young, hip, and fresh.

Nicole, I'm so glad that the universe brought our souls together (again)! Your energy, positivity, and zest for life continue to make me so happy. You are sunshine in human form, so much so that I've stopped taking my vitamin D supplements.

Kennedy, thank you for your beautiful lens on the world, your keen eye for graphic design, and for being such an awesome supportive human being.

Elizabeth, thank you for leaning into my teal obsession and styling me with the most gorgeous hues of blue power pajama suits, and for your passion for all things marketing. The universe knew what it was doing bringing you into our lives. You're stuck with us!

To our hilarious team of twenty-two improv professionals who bring laughter, levity, and positivity to companies across the world, this book would not exist without your belief in the vision of *improve it!* Your humor and deep empathy for those around you make every plane ride and every road trip the best day ever. I'm deeply grateful for your commitment to this company and have endless gratitude for a team that shares so much love.

To the amazing clients we get to serve (over 400 of you!), thank you for trusting us, believing in our work, and allowing us to bring our love of improv comedy to your offices. It is an honor and a privilege to work with people who truly care for the people they lead.

To every participant who has chicken danced in one of our workshops or who has "won the lottery" with me in one of our keynotes, thank you for being my *why*. Watching you get comfortable with the uncomfortable and be the person you were meant to be is my life's purpose.

To the amazing *improve it!* peeps who tune into the *improve it!* podcast week after week. We are growing, learning, and failing together at this thing called life. Keep doing it, because you know that the world needs that special *it* that only you can bring!

Additionally, I would not be writing this book without the help of people who coach and mentor me. Jane Atkinson, my speaking coach and incredible mentor, thank you for pushing me and guiding me on this keynote speaker and author journey.

To Michael Frontier, my intuitive coach, you have changed my life in so many ways. Thank you for listening, for allowing me to throw daggers at you when you didn't deserve it (OK, they weren't real daggers, but you created a safe space for my pain), and for always guiding me to be the best version of my highest self.

I also want to thank my forever inspiration and constant source of female empowerment, Judi Holler, for guiding me to the incredible team at Greenleaf and for being the mentor and friend every female entrepreneur needs. I love watching you stand in your power. You inspire me more than you know.

Greenleaf, let me swear for the first time in this book. Y'all are the shit! Justin Branch, thank you for believing in me and giving me all the feels in our first meeting. Brian Welch, you are the most detailed and thoughtful project manager I could ask for. Tess Newton, the universe knew what it was doing pairing the two of us together. Thank you for listening to my vision, guiding the tone of this book, and believing in it wholeheartedly. I see you! Nathan True, it is TRUE that you and I will be friends for life. You are a fantastic editor, and I'm so grateful for you putting up with my puns and desire to tell stories through humor. Tenyia Lee, thank you for your edits and wonderful words. Anna Jordan, thank you for your patience with a recovering perfectionist and for creating the perfect book cover. And to the many people behind the scenes not mentioned—a million hugs for your belief in this project!

To my friends, who believe in me, support me, and show up every single day. Thank you for witnessing all my improv shows (even the cringy bad ones in the beginning); letting me write poems for your weddings, birthdays, and celebrations; and allowing me to be my true, wacky, weird self. I would not be who I am without your love and constant support. You know who you are!

To the Diehl family, who has embraced my flawesome, spontaneous, eclectic ways into their own with the upmost love. I love you all so much, and my world is infinitely better with all of you in it.

To Callie Sphatt, thank you for filling our home with sunshine and our son with Taylor Swift lyrics. You are a part of our family forever, and we would not, could not, do life without you.

And if you've gotten this far in the book, you know I'm a bit "woo woo," and I would be nothing without my spiritual practice. Thank you to my guides, my angels, and the team who is helping me stay in "alignment with my assignment" here on Earth School. I promise to fulfill my soul's purpose and do the work. You have my word.

Finally, I am forever grateful to my husband, John. You are my Earth angel, my best friend, my soul mate, and I am the luckiest person on the planet to have you by my side. You make every day more fun, thoughtful, and adventurous, and I don't know who or what I would be without you. I'm so grateful to you and to the amazing human we brought to life, Jackson Diehl.

Jackson (a.k.a. Goose), you are my—and our—greatest creation. Your kindness, empathy, humor, and compassion are my life's greatest gifts. I'm so proud of who you are. Thank you for being my biggest teacher. I love you and will always and forever SEE YOU.

About the Author

Erin "Big" Diehl is a business improv edutainer, failfluencer, and keynote speaker. Through a series of unrelated dares, Erin created *improve it!*—a unique professional development company that uses improvisational comedy and experiential learning to sharpen leaders and teams so they can thrive in ever-changing environments and do it with a whole lot of laughs along the way.

Erin is a graduate of Clemson University, a former experiential marketing and recruiting professional, and a veteran improviser from the top improvisational training programs in Chicago, including The Second City, iO Theater, and The Annoyance Theater.

Having spoken on global stages with companies like Amazon, LinkedIn, and the Obama Foundation, Erin has an energy and message to share with the world that creates lasting ripple effects for change. As a graduate of the Goldman Sachs 10,000 Small Business Program and member of The Chicago Innovation Awards Women's Cohort, Erin is a living testament to the power of lifelong learning and how working to understand ourselves helps others to do so, too.

Erin is the proud host of a top 1 percent global podcast, *The improve it! Podcast*, which you can find anywhere you listen to pods! Among her many accolades, Erin is most proud of successfully coercing over 35,000 professionals to chicken dance. When she's not playing pretend or facilitating, she enjoys being outside with her husband, son, and eight-pound toy poodle, BIGG DIEHL.

Call Me, Maybe?!

Hey Carly Rae Jepsen fans (OK, maybe you're not a fan, but you have to know this song). Did you see yourself in this book? (Pun always intended.) If you feel connected to the content, then let's connect in real life! Here are all the ways we can continue this Energy U curriculum for years to come!

1. Let's get social: Follow me on all social channels @itserindiehl. I live mostly on Instagram, Facebook, LinkedIn, and TikTok.

   - @itserindiehl
   - Erin Diehl Keynote Speaker
   - linkedin.com/in/erindiehl
   - @itserindiehl

2. Listen and subscribe to *The* improve it! *Podcast*: Every week, I drop a new episode to help you develop yourself into the best version of YOU possible, so you can develop your team and lead with intentionality, transparency, and authenticity. I'll give you more tips and tools that have helped me on my own personal journey and combine that with the wisdom and expertise of our fantastic guests. Oversharing and knee-slappers guaranteed.

QR code to take you right to Apple Podcasts

3. Sign up for our F.A.I.L. Friday newsletter: Find a signup link right on the homepage of my website, www.itserindiehl.com. Every Friday, you'll receive a fun compilation of #fails, awakenings, ideas, and laughs straight to your inbox. It's a great way to end the week!

4. Finally, if you want to really connect in real life—let's meet in person! You can hire me to keynote speak at your next conference or convention or hire the amazing improv professionals at *improve it!* to provide a power skill building workshop for your team. We've worked with everyone from the Fortune 100 to small and mid-size businesses to transform their team and their people through play! Let us improve your "it," whatever your "it" may be! You can find out more and connect at www.itserindiehl.com.